The purpose of this book is to acquaint teachers, child psychologists, child psychiatrists, community workers and other interested professionals and para-professionals with the problems of disturbed children and the ways in which these problems are handled in a range of circumstances. It is intended to provide a broad perspective on children's emotional problems with ideas and practices from specialists divergent in both training and theoretical positions.

The book is case-oriented with a representative range of treatment settings and therapeutic viewpoints. Ten cases, from four to seventeen years, present a variety of problems over a range of mild to severe. Every case is written by the person who played the key roles in servicing the case. This makes the cases engaging and the discussions practical. The book is, however, more than case studies for it includes two chapters and relatively elaborate case introductions designed to cover general issues, highlight theoretical problems and place each case presented in context with the overall purpose of the book.

DISTURBED AND TROUBLED CHILDREN

Disturbed and Troubled Children

EDITED BY

MAURICE F. FREEHILL

University of Washington, Seattle

With assistance from the late Barbara B. Hauck

SPECTRUM PUBLICATIONS, INC.
Flushing, New York

Distributed by Halsted Press
A DIVISION OF JOHN WILEY & SONS
New York   Toronto   London   Sydney

Spectrum Publications, Inc. 75-31 192 St., Flushing, N.Y. 11366.

Distributed solely by Halsted Press, a Division of John Wiley & Sons, Inc., New York.

Library of Congress Cataloging in Publication Data

Freehill, Maurice F.
  Disturbed and Troubled Children

1. Mentally ill children—Addresses, essays, lectures. 2. Problem children—Addresses, essays, lectures. I. Title. (DNLM: 1. Affective disturbances—In infancy & childhood—Case studies. 2. Child behavior disorders—Case Studies. WS350
F855d 1973)
RJ499.F75   371.9′4   73–12465
ISBN 0–470–27736–X

This volume is dedicated to Barbara B. Hauck who died while the manuscript was in preparation. She was a gifted colleague and an advocate for exceptional children

Contributors

WILLIAM B. BURLINGAME, Ph.D., University of North Carolina, and Director, Adolescent Unit, John Umstead Hospital, Butner, North Carolina

DIANA F. DAVIS, Ph.D., Psychologist and Lecturer in Education, Monash University, Clayton, Australia

WILLIAM M. EASSON, M.D., Chairman, Department of Psychiatry, Medical College of Ohio, Toledo, Ohio

ROBERT T. ELLIOTT, Ed.D., Director, Center for Psychological, and Educational Services, Sacramento, California

MAURICE F. FREEHILL, Ed.D., Chairman, Department of Educational Psychology, University of Washington, Seattle, Washington

BARBARA B. HAUCK, Ph.D. (deceased), University of Washington, Seattle, Washington

HAROLD J. LOCKETT, M.D., Assistant Director, Hawthorn Center, Northville, Michigan

ESTHER MARINE, Ph.D., Chief, Psychiatric Social Work, Pittsburgh Child Guidance Center, Pittsburgh, Pennsylvania

EVELYN P. MASON, Ph.D., Western State College, Bellingham, Washington

WILLIAM C. MORSE, Ph.D., University of Michigan, Ann Arbor, Michigan

MADELINE F. REID, B.A., A.T.T.I., Psychologist and Senior Guidance Officer, Department of Education, Victoria, Australia

DENNIS H. STOTT, Ph.D., Director, Center for Educational Disabilities, University of Guelph, Ontario, Canada

JEAN D. WICKLUND, M.D., Clinical Instructor, University of Washington, Seattle, Washington

Contents

CHAPTER 1

Disturbed and Troubled Children

MAURICE F. FREEHILL

The purpose of this book is to acquaint teachers, community workers, workers in child psychiatry and psychology and parents with the problems of disturbed children and the ways in which these problems are handled in a range of circumstances. The first chapter provides a general perspective and the remainder of the book reports on specific cases in special settings: school, clinic, hospital, or residential center. Hopefully, the case studies approach builds not only awareness and knowledge but commitment to troubled and troublesome children. At least these cases show the crucial effects that come with care from one knowledgeable adult.

"Disturbed" is an umbrella term. It includes disturbing and socially deviant cases as well as maladjusted and anxious ones. The disturbance may be primary or it may be an accompaniment of some generic physical or social problem. The label "disturbed" is applied sometimes to groups but more often to cases and these vary greatly—compulsive sufferers, disrupters, deviant believers, victims of milieu stress, or unsteady workers. "Disturbed" is an inclusive and untidy category but it

1

has two practical superiorities; it discourages terminal prescriptive management and it brings to attention many children who would be excluded under narrower and more exact definitions.

HOW MANY AND WHO ARE THEY?

The trend is to discard nosology (the systematic classification of illness) and use instead an open, working description of personal-interpersonal behavior including many common and less than pathologic problems. In the following chapters, diagnosis is rarely viewed as a special or isolated phase ending in either a once-only categorization or an explicit prescription. The case authors treat assessment as a continuous process, an integrated part of working with the client. This functional and changing assessment combines with low reliability of measurement, irregularity in the manifestations of stress, and recessions through natural events to create very wide variance in estimates of the numbers who are maladjusted.

From teacher ratings on elementary children, Wickman (1928) estimated 42 percent mild and 7 percent seriously maladjusted. Carl Rogers (1942) found 33 percent mild and 12 percent severe for elementary children in Columbus, Ohio. Other surveys find proportions from 12.9 percent in Northwest Tennessee in 1968 to approximately one-third elsewhere (31 percent) in an upper middle class group in New York, 30 percent in Chicago, and about one-third in Rochester, N.Y. (Glavin, 1967; Glidwell and Swallow, 1969; Cowen, 1971). In 1969, a psychiatrically oriented report from the Joint Commission on Mental Health of Children considered 2 percent of all under 25 years in need of psychiatric care with a further 8 percent needing other special help (Joint Commission on Mental Health of Children, 1970).

From reviewing the data, White and Harris (1961) concluded that a figure for mild disturbance was impractical but a working estimate for serious maladjustment was between 2 and 12 percent. A practical and widely used rate comes from Bower (1960) in California: 10 percent emotionally handicapped and 2 or 3 percent in urgent need of help.

This variance in findings reflects both problems of reliability and the mixing of development with school performance. In 1928, Wickman assumed that teachers' judgments of mental health problems erred if they deviated from psychiatric diagnoses. Subsequent studies reported increasing agreement between teachers' and mental health specialists' judgments, the result of modification from both sides. Teachers became attentive to personality development while mental health specialists increased attention to the relation between accomplishment and adjustment. Criteria for child mental health include elements of learning, achievement, and growth both because teachers are involved in evaluation and because these are prime tasks of childhood.

There is a low and irregular correlation between adjustment and achievement. The first case in the first American clinic was referred for a school learning problem and was a male. Boys continue to dominate most clinical samples, often at a level of 2:1 and they commonly have reading, behavior, or speech problems (Bower, 1960; Bentzen, 1963; Cowen, 1971). The peak age of referral is earlier for boys than for girls, more nearly coincident with stabilization of school failure and with attainment of size and strength adequate to support antisocial feelings.

It is doubtful, however, that there is one single or separate general relation between achievement and adjustment. A study of 310, 11 year-olds found complex interrelations between type of anxiety and type of achievement with some correlations holding for one sex but not the other (Frost, 1968). Emotional dysfunction is complex. Single symptoms or single life conditions are inadequate either to predict breakdown or to serve as evidence of emotional disorder. Disturbance appears reciprocally related to family conflict, perceptual distortion, disruptive behavior, speech defects, and other factors which are in turn complementary one to another.

It seems established that reading-disabled pupils have adjustment problems but it is less certain that emotionally disturbed children have reading problems. Reading and mathematics deficiencies are found in both institutionalized and out-patient populations (Shimota, 1964). In one study, reading disability rates were 10 percent in school, 13 percent in a guidance clinic, 63 percent in a placement agency, 73 percent in a children's psychiatric hospital and 83 percent in a clinic serving deprived delinquents (Fabian, 1955). Educational deficits often accompany emotional disturbance but not in such a straightforward, one-to-one pattern.

One investigator divided disturbed children into five problem groups and found that the "neurotic-psychotic" were most efficient and the "school difficulties" least efficient in reading and arithmetic (Schroeder, 1965). In another study, 2200 children, 9 to 11 years old, were screened and 284 nominated as possible maladjusteds. Following interviews, 126 were believed to have clinically important disorders. Seventeen boys and 26 girls were classified "neurotic", 64 boys and 5 girls were classified "antisocial". There was a strong association of poor reading with "antisocial" but not with "neurotic" (Yule and Rutter, 1968). It is quite unclear whether the reading failures were an outcome of being male, antisocial, or both, or of some unexamined factors. In reverse, it is possible that reading failure was a prime reason for becoming antisocial. The term "emotional disturbance" is global but not homogeneous and different patterns of disturbance have different correlations with academic performance.

Behaviors related to learning difficulty are somewhat alike whether found in poorly adjusted or well-adjusted children. *A Behavior Rating Scale for Junior-Senior High School* (Swift and Spivack, 1969) was evolved from teachers' ratings on academic behaviors. One hundred and two items were reduced to 13 factors. Twelve of these were significantly related to achievement in 882 children from Chester County, Pa. and all 13 were significantly related for 672 children in residential treatment at Devereux Schools. Undoubtedly teachers over-attend to disruptive behavior, but several studies show that they make reliable discriminations based on classroom observations (Walsh and O'Connor, 1968; Werry and Quay, 1969; Nelson, 1971). It has long been practice to depend on teachers for a first screening and in contemporary services the teacher plays a longer and more active role.

Increased use of classroom observations and teacher opinion comes both from enlarged definitions of mental health and in response to shortcomings in clinic diagnosis. Extended observation in normal situations gives attention to a full display of behavior, thereby supplementing clinical examination. Cooperative diagnosis also enhances the probability that recommendations will be practical and acceptable. Pupil questionnaires and guide questions for nonclinical assessments prove useful when employed as a screen or for a specific purpose (Stott, 1960; Kvaraceus, 1961). They make exceedingly modest contributions to any detailed understanding of an individual (Lessing and Smouse, 1967).

To involve teachers in diagnoses, causes uneasiness among people who view schools as instruments of a partisan faction in society. Less-established groups claim education is coercive and educators are unable to comprehend or accept ethnic, social, and value differences. It is agreed that culture shapes symptomatology and confuses diagnosis. Confusion may account for some of the elevated ratios and categorical differences reported for disadvantaged and minority groups (Yablonsky, 1962; Walsh and O'Connor, 1968; Kappelman,

Kaplan and Ganter, 1969). These differences also reflect delay of referral for working class children even when they are causing significant teacher concern (McDermott, Harrison, Schrager, and Wilson, 1965). Naturally, problems deepen in the additional time and may be differently manifested at different ages.

Early studies concentrated on correlations between social or personality defects and socioeconomic class as defined by fathers' occupation, parents' level of education, etc. Socioeconomic class is so conglomerate that recent studies have examined more specific child rearing and family variables. The findings demonstrate differences in learning style, externality, and forms of social interaction (Miller and Swanson, 1960; Battle and Rotter, 1963). For the most part, clinics fail to treat effectively the same persons that schools fail to teach (White, 1965). Both agencies make special efforts and some of these are described in four cases of alienated or ethnically isolated children found in in this volume.

Identification procedures that are field-based and incorporate teacher and lay ratings will uncover a large number of cases, but many of these will be transient disorders or examples of near normal stress. An investigation of 482 randomly selected children in Buffalo, N.Y., shows that mothers reported many symptomatic behaviors (thumb-sucking, nail-biting, tics, bedwetting, etc). More of these were reported for younger children and for children in low socioeconomic families but correlations with adjustment were minimal (Lapouse, 1966). Some symptoms that worry mothers are associated with transient or developmental problems. Nevertheless, elementary and high school records do show significant relation to nursery school reports on matters of family deviation, the child's relationships with peers, and eccentric behavior (Westman Rice and Berman, 1967). Retrospective study finds that approximately one-quarter of teachers' comments in first grade are predictive of adjustment in seventh (Zax, Cowen, Rappaport, Beach, and Laird, 1968).

The best known follow-up was reported by Robbins (1966). Five hundred and twenty-five clinic children were compared with 100 controls 30 years later. Only 20 percent were free of psychiatric disease while 52 percent of controls enjoyed that status. Thirty-four percent of clinic graduates and only 8 percent of controls had disabling symptoms. The most persistent effects were not shy or neurotic tendencies but antisocial behaviors. Brown (1963) reported on 105 boys and 31 girls from the greater Boston area, diagnosed as atypical (infantile psychosis) in preschool years. The minimum age at follow-up report was 9 years and eight percent were 19 or more. Most had received treatment and 37 percent were near age-level in learning but 27 percent had no record of academic achievement. Fifty-four percent appeared able to function in society although only 5 percent appeared "normal" with 23 percent "neurotic" and 26 percent "schizoid". The remaining 46 percent needed some form of protective or custodial care. In this group, the severity of problems at the time of diagnosis was of prime significance in predicting later well-being.

A summary of studies gives support to the belief that disturbed children do more often become problem adults but there are numerous remissions particularly among children without additional handicaps (Clarizio, 1968). Shy, inhibited, or neurotic problems fade more than acting-out or antisocial ones but the probability of overcoming either is correlated with mildness in the original condition. It is essential to recognize that these children grown-up have a wide range of functioning.

ANXIETY AND LEARNING

The Yerkes-Dodson principle dating from 1908, has generally been accepted as proof that emotion and stress serve to enhance learning to some optimal level but thereafter increments of stress are associated with decrements in learning. The inverted U effect is interpreted to mean that children may be under-aroused, efficiently aroused, or over-aroused. The latter state either introduces new task elements or dissipates attention. High-anxious subjects may have success in simple or repetitive tasks but decline in competence as difficulty or threat increases. Beyond this, there is evidence that anxiety-prone groups regularly respond in patterns like these produced by situational anxiety (Smock, 1962). If we assume that anxiety is more pervasive with disturbed children and if they are more susceptible to periodic floods of stress, then they are more consistently the victims of drives which go beyond efficiency toward panic.

A somewhat different but not essentially contradictory model might be called the Spence-Eysenck explanation in which anxiety serves a mediating function or is an acquired drive. The task or "to-be-learned" response is weak so that high drive promotes competing responses until practice has strengthened the desired response. So it is, that high drive inhibits novel or complex learning (Taylor and Spence, 1952; Lipman and Griffith, 1960). This view fits neatly with Eysenck's statement (1965) that individuals differ in hereditary reactivity, with reactives and high-conditionables prone to neurotic responses, while extroverted, low-conditionables are potentially poorly socialized or psychopathic. Extroverts develop reactive inhibition and fail to learn routine and conformity behavior.

Numerous studies give substance to this position. Achieving students in Britain were found to be steady workers sustained by anxiety and introversion (Lynn, 1959). This is the expected state of affairs when educational tasks are repetitive, conforming, and memoriter. The other end of the continuum was demonstrated with 200 freshmen at the University of North Carolina. It was low-anxious students who performed best in "flexibility," "alternate-uses," and "consequences tests" (White, 1968).

The findings are muddied by evidence of influences from sex, ability, situational, and experience variables. In general, high scores on the *Children's Manifest Anxiety Scale* or the anxiety measure from the *Affect Adjective List* are correlated with low curiousity, low willingness to seek stimulation, and poor concomitant memory (Silverman, 1954; Zuckerman, Kolin, Price and Zoob, 1964; Penny, 1965). There are both research and day-to-day indications that some people handle stress effectively but in most cases stress restricts experience either by reducing participation or targeting activity in repetitive fashion. Anxious children perform best on assignments with few alternative responses (Pickerel, 1958). Their largest deficits are in learning what is original, humane, or complex.

Experiments show that high-anxious children are more than normally dependent on the quality of reinforcements. They, of course, live with fewer positive reflections and less regular reward. The reader of this volume will scarcely escape the conclusion that the quality of approval and the distribution of parental attention was faulty for Jerry, Kristen, Helen, Ken, and Mike.

Assessed on longevity and extent of use, the anxiety construct would appear to have demonstrated both validity and usefulness. Nevertheless, many modern behaviorists dismiss the construct as erroneous, or useless, or both. They reject special explanations and contend that behavior depends not on rational or irrational processes but on environmental consequences. For them, neurosis is neither a special defense against impulse nor a disguised release of passion, but is instead maladaptive behavior learned, elicited, and maintained by contingencies in the environment. At most, anxiety is behavior reinforced by escape or reinforced because it reduces contact with fearful or noxious stimuli and the quality of incomprehensibility about it arises because innocent experience or neutral stimulus was once paired with fright or aversive stimulus but now we fail to perceive what connects benign elements with terror.

(It makes an immense difference if disturbed children are viewed as simply maladapted, having either bad) habits or a shortage of useful habits—a condition which may be straight-forwardly remediated. Then projective testing or searching for meanings in behavior and symptoms gives way to diagnosis which compares the emitted against the desired responses. Then, too, there is no need to arouse inhibited impulses, develop new or stronger identifications, or wait on a growing core of meaning and value. The action therapist, having established a contemporary baseline and behavioral goals, subdivides the intermediate ground into learning tasks and attacks these in order using the tactics of conditioning, counterconditioning, and contingency management. Most case reports in this volume use an anxiety idea but they avoid categorical diagnosis and use sociologic or learning explanations.

CONTEMPORARY PERSPECTIVES

The interpretation of case materials may be assisted by a brief examination of theories and special concerns which influence modern practice.

Active Developmental View

In the last 15 years, attention shifted from repression and deficiency to development and achievement, away from rescue efforts toward assisted growth. There is less total concern with easing agonies and lifting repression and more with teaching interpersonal skills and autonomy. This change fits the new realities. Under the influence of Spock, Freud, and others, contemporary adults have become less repressive and children now indulge in abundant, if sometimes graceless, expressions of impulse.

The repression idea is most persistent in diagnosis. It

is a rare psychologist who would fail to note that one client doodles soft container-like forms while another sketches firm horn-like shapes. Reading failures among intelligent children are often interpreted as passive-aggressive payback for parental insults. Most therapeutic workers see seductive messages in family conversation or find signs of passion in painting or they believe that mannerisms assumed by an "artiste" are interpretable as mimics of prohibited acts (McClelland, 1963).

The dictum that "mental illness is like any other illness" was useful in energizing public funding, but it has become an embarrassment. Early disaffection came from laymen who believed mental health activities interfered with the development of character and morality. Then in the early 1960's, Thomas Szasz (1961) and other professionals made sharp distinctions between biologic or infectious disease and the inability to function within social norms.

The medical model assumed that there was an underlying cause with symptomatic manifestations and that diagnosis, treatment, and cure were directed toward a relatively dependent patient. In the replacement or psychological model, the problem is maladaptive or unsuitable behavior learned by deficits in training and maintained by rewards or by the avoidance of pain, and correction is achieved through the ordinary rules of learning (Ullman and Krasner, 1965). This change is not simply from analytic to behavioristic thinking. Modern analysts or ego-psychologists make a very similar distinction. Eli Bower (1966) contrasts intrapsychic and social competency models. The intrapsychic goal is *emotional freedom* which is measured subjectively and achieved through a program of self-understanding. The social competency goal is *effective transaction* with the environment which is measured by a fitness in personal function and achieved through programs that are task-centered.

A focus on growth and prevention reduces attention

to what is dramatic and extreme. The reader will find that the majority of cases in this volume seem near-normal.

Sociological Emphasis

It is an old idea that the individual is either deeply influenced by or is a product of social structure. It is often said that an automated industrial society processes people to become robots. American individualism was replaced by organization men through the rise of a technological and corporate system. The accepted myth was "progress through production." Many mature people join with youth in feeling that they have been dispossessed into a world of abundance but cheated out of excitement, adventure, and personal meaning. Dissenters claim that progress came at too high a price, that we secured products at the price of self-realization and technical development at the cost of ecological and cultural devastation. The competitive society seemed to reduce tenderness and intimacy and many people proposed a new and more personal lifestyle with feelings assigned a powerful role in the conduct of thought and life.

Freud tended to neglect sociological factors but in *Civilization and Its Discontents* he did address himself to what he believed was an inevitable conflict between person and society. Others now view analytic theory as a fundamental departure point for structuring a new society. The student movement which came late in America has been described as a reworking of father-son conflicts (Feuer, 1969). School, law, and government are father-like authorities and conflict with them is energized by old and compulsive family feelings. In this view, it is archaic impulse which causes the "established" group to repress the new generation and it is also impulse which leads students to reject a social order developed by their fathers and to force confrontation even in a very permissive environment.

We may believe that counter-culture is shaped by subconscious guides or we may think it is the product of dissonant social expectations with limited opportunities for affiliative experience and social apprenticeship. In any case, alienation and disaffection are found at every level of ability. One example is found in the case of Jerry (chapter 10). Many of his generation feel powerless in their own lives and as a consequence, they wound or withdraw. Passivity or aggression is often related to school failure but encompasses the landscape of life.

Studies of classroom climate show that many children "tune-out" and this includes both the achieving and underachieving (Nordstrom, Freidenberg and Gold, 1967; Jackson, 1968). Boredom and noninvolvement extend beyond the schools. There is a developing psychiatric view that going mad is one of a few sane options available in a disordered society. What is called "maladaptive" may be a special strategy for life in a defective society and forms of deviance may be especially chosen to communicate need although the message is often avoided when observers classify the behavior as either dangerous or inferior (Halleck, 1971a).

The sociological emphasis has supported an increasing concern with socioeconomic, racial, and ethnic differences. At least two of the following cases make underprivilege and minority status central issues. Experts undertaking study of individuals find themselves turning to an evaluation of society (Fyvel, 1961). They are pained by the concentration and the permanence of handicapping conditions and some have concluded that mental health services are of little value in an impoverished or racist society. Some of these politicize mental health and shift from serving individuals to modifying society with professionals becoming advocates, organizers, and campaigners (Halleck, 1971b).

Mental health became a public problem with each case to be handled in an arena larger than a mental hospital or clinic office. In support of the Community Mental Health Centers Act in 1963, the President, John Kennedy, said:

> If we launch a broad new mental health program now, it will be possible within a decade or two to reduce the number of patients now under custodial care by fifty percent or more. Many more mentally ill can be helped to remain in their own homes without hardship to themselves or their families. Those who are hospitalized can be helped to return to their communities. All but a small proportion can be restored to useful life. We can spare them and their families much of the misery which mental illness now entails. We can save public funds and we can conserve our manpower resources.

As community mental health centers developed they established a variety of relations with schools. Both agencies conceived their task in broad general services more than explicitly therapeutic programs. In community centers, and to some degree in schools, services are offered in several locations and by people with varied professional backgrounds. Use was made of aides and volunteers. The arguments for employment of lay helpers are: economy, the preference for work in nearby settings and the belief that laymen will cross communication barriers with minorities and inner city groups (Sobey, 1970).

Divergent Psychological Models

Special education literature is dominated by two models, the analytic and behavioral. The relation between the two has been acrimonious with behaviorists insisting that observable behavior is the only important variable and there is no need to deal with an "unconscious" and its specialized psychological laws. For the behaviorist, there is but one set of rules: personality is a matter of conditioning history and not the outcome of a special pleasure principle. Salter (1961) says that the person is normal for what happened to him, "maladjustment is malconditioning and psychotherapy is reconditioning." Extreme critics have called psychoanalysis a hoax (Pinckney and Pinckney, 1965). On the other side, Norman Cameron (1963), an analyst, had this to say:

> One who neglects these furious fancies and mental ghosts and shadows, will never gain a deep and therapeutically helpful understanding of the true mechanisms that underlie mental life. From the psychodynamic point of view of this book the behavioristic approach to psychopathology mentioned above is not a study of the real mind of man but it is rather a point of view that assumes that man is, in fact, not a living human being but an inanimate computer.

The sharpness of this exchange is probably a result of theoretical proximity or similarity. In the extreme, both are deterministic, reductionist, and closed systems. Recent gains in popularity are on the behaviorist side with many advocates of precision teaching, operant conditioning, engineered classrooms, or behavior modification. We cannot here deal with counter claims or evaluation of views but in simple terms behaviorists claim to individuate instruction or treatment by not limiting themselves to a single diagnostic tool or a single therapeutic method. They hope to discover events or conditions which alter the behavior of a particular person and then deal with that behavior directly, not inferentially (Gaasholt, 1970; Lovitt, 1970). The method is at its best with clients who have few options, when the therapist has maximum control over the use of time and rewards (Mainord, 1968). Reports include many institutionalized cases and studies of children which center on developing acceptable social behavior in retardates or reducing antisocial behavior in delinquents (Phillips, Fixen and Wolf, 1973).

All of this does not imply the abandonment of psychodynamic practices. A number of well established treatment centers are analytic and new uses periodically emerge. Several new counseling trends are closely hinged to analytic concepts and there has been sharp interest in work with schizophrenics started by Morris and Jacqui Schiff employing a total patient regression followed by the development of a substitute parent-child relation and an extended therapeutic experience with a second growing-up (Schiff, 1969).

School counselors are a first line of service for disturbed children and counseling views are often rooted in depth or analytic psychology and then influenced by perceptual and self-actualization theories. The counseling viewpoint has been expanded into a full educational perspective with emphasis on student concerns and process, called psychological, humanistic, affective, personalogic, or eupsychian education (Rogers, 1969; Borton, 1970).

There are a multitude of deviations in new viewpoints. They include human potentials institutes, expanding human awareness, conjoint family therapy and gestalt groups, supplemented by transpersonal association, yoga, I-Ching, and Zen as well as physicalist approaches such as bioenergetics, the Alexander technique, and Rolfing. Recent radical criticism claims that traditional or professional training and selection makes counselors inept, self-enhancing, and committed to the status quo (Lewis and Dworkin, 1971). The critics propose a people-organized, people-to-people help center. Parents who spend days going the rounds to seek help for troubled children must surely find a mass of jig-saw pieces.

The authors of this volume make many joinings between models. Nevertheless, each operates from some central or powerful assumptions and these modify the principles that are brought in. The higher level concept or organizing idea is not accounted for by the subsumed generalizations much as vocabulary is not determined by phonics or art is not determined by the rules of perspective.

Culture-Specific Concerns

Individual alienation and social discord are contemporary concerns. Many people of every age and every social class report boredom and a sense of impotence in the massive, bureaucratic society.

Many mental health workers in every role are concerned about drug abuse. There is an increase in quantity and variety of substances used as stimulants with limited agreement on how to handle the phenomenon (Louria, 1968; Clark and Funkhouser, 1970). It seems likely that new chemical and mechanical agents will be available to modify behavior (London, 1971). Some authorities believe that an overuse of prescriptive psychoactives is an outcome of the medical model in psychological thought (Rogers, 1971). There is some evidence that symptoms of assaultive, self-injuring, insomniac, or hyperactive natures are reduced through pharmacology, but there is little information on long-run effects (Leonard, 1969; Lucas and Pasley, 1969; Faretra, Dooher and Dowling, Sprague, Barnes and Werry, 1970). Does the use of drugs reduce disruptiveness but also the motivation for solving vital problems? Does the use of psychoactive prescriptions teach a defective attitude about self and self-management?

Problems of poverty and social disorder have high visibility. It is clear that academic and personal growth are directly related to soecioeconomic conditions, parental levels of education and accomplishment, and to the attention and affection received from teachers. Modern helping agencies—Model Cities, New Careers, schools, Head Start, and community mental health—share common goals and are interested in almost identical target populations. They try to provide relevant and enlarged developmental opportunities for minorities, stigmatized groups, alienated, and low self-regarding children and youth.

References

Battle, E.S., and Rotter, J.B. (1963). "Children's feelings of personal control as related to social class and ethnic group," *Journal of Personality, 31,* 483–490.

Bentzen, F. (1963). "Sex ratios in learning and behavior disorders," *American Journal of Orthopsychiatry, 33* (1), 92–98.

Borton T. (1970) Reach Touch, and Teach, *New York: McGraw-Hill.*

Bower, E.M. (1960). *Early Identification of Emotionally Handicapped Children in Schools,* Springfield, Ill.: Thomas.

Bower, E.M. (1966). "The achievement of competency," in R.R. Leeper, (Ed.) *Learning and Mental Health in the School,* Washington, D.C.: Association for Supervision and Curriculum Development, N.E.A. 23–46.

Brown, J.L. (1963). "Follow-up of children with atypical development (infantile psychosis)," *American Journal of Orthopsychiatry, 23,* 855–861.

Cameron, N. (1963) *Personality Development and Psychopathology: A Dynamic Approach,* Boston. Houghton Mifflin, vii–viii.

Clarizio, H. (1968). "Stability of deviant behavior through time," *Mental Hygiene, 52,* 288–293.

Clark, W.H., and Funkhouser, G.R. (1970) "Physicians and researchers disagree on psychedelic drugs," *Psychology Today, 11,* 48–50, 70–73.

Cowan, E.L. (1971). "Emergent directions in school mental health," *American Scientist, 59* (6), 723–733.

Eysenck, H.J. (1965). *Fact and Fiction in Psychology,* London: Penguin.

Fabian, A.A. (1955). "Reading disability: an index to pathology," *American Journal of Orthopsychiatry, 25,* 319–329.

Faretra, G., Dooher, L., Dowling, J. (1970) "Comparison of haloperidal and fluphenazine in disturbed children," *American Journal of Psychiatry, 126,* 1670–1673.

Feuer, L.S. (1969) *The Conflict of Generations: The Character and Significance of Student Movements,* New York: Basic Books.

Frost, B.P. (1968). "Anxiety and educational achievement," *British Journal of Educational Psychology, 38,* 293–301.

Fyvel, T.R. (1961). *Troublemakers: Rebellious youth in an affluent society,* New York: Schocken.

Gaasholt, M. (1970). "Precision techniques in the management of teacher and child behaviors," *Exceptional Children, 37* (2), 129–135.

Glavin, J.P. (1967). "Spontaneous improvement in emotionally disturbed children," doctoral thesis, George Peabody College for Teachers, Nashville, Tenn.

Glidwell, J.C., and Swallow, C.S. (1969). *The Prevalence of Maladjustment in Elementary Schools,* Chicago: Chicago University Press.

Halleck, S. (1971a). "Therapy is the handmaiden of the status quo," *Psychology Today, 4* (11), 30–34, 98–100.

Halleck, S. (1971b). "The uses of abnormality," *Current, 31,* 43–50.

Jackson, P.W. (1968) *Life in Classrooms,* New York: Holt, Rinehart and Winston, 40–111.

Joint Commission on Mental Health of Children (1970). *Crisis in Child Mental Health: Challenge for the 1970's,* New York: Harper and Row, 38–39.

Kappelman, M.M., Kaplan, E., Ganter, R.F., (1969). "A study of learning disorders among disadvantaged children," *Journal of Learning Disabilities, 2,* 262–268.

Kennedy, J.F. (1963). "Mental illness and mental retardation," message to the House of Representatives, 88th Congress, February 5.

Kvaraceus, W.C. (1961). "Forecasting juvenile delinquency: a three-year experiment," *Exceptional Children, 28,* 429–435.

Lapouse, R. (1966). "The epidemiology of behavior disorders in children," *American Journal of Diseases of Children, 3,* 594–599.

Leonard, J. (1969). "Haloperidal in the treatment of behavior disorders in children and adolescents," *Canadian Psychiatric Association Journal, 14,* 217–220.

Lessing, E.E. and Smouse, A.D. (1967). "Use of children's personality questionnaire in differentiating between normal and disturbed children," *Educational and Psychological Measurement, 27, 659–669.*

Lewis, M.D., Lewis, J.A., and Dworkin, E.P. (eds.) (1971). *The Personnel and Guidance Journal, 49* (9).

Lipman, R.S., and Griffith, B.C. (1960). "Effects of anxiety level on concept formation: a test of drive theory," *American Journal of Mental Deficiency, 65,* 342–348.

London, P. (1971). *Behavior Control: The Danger and the Promise,* New York: Harper and Row (A Perennial Library Book).

Louria, D.B. (1968) *The Drug Scene,* New York: McGraw-Hill.

Lovitt, T. (1970). "Behavior modification: the current scene," *Exceptional Children, 37* (2), 85–91.

Lucas, A.R., and Pasley, F.C. (1969). "Psycho-active drugs in the treatment of emotionally disturbed children: haloperidal and diazipam," *Comprehensive Psychiatry, 10,* 376–386.

Lynn, R. (1959) "Two personality characteristics related to academic achievement," *British Journal of Educational Psychology, 29,* 213–216.

Mainord, W.A. (1968). "Operant group therapy in a total instruction setting," *The Discoverers, 6.*

McClelland, D.C. (1963). "On the psychodynamics of creative physical scientists," in H.E. Gruber, Terrell, G. and Wertheimer, M., Eds., *Contemporary Approaches to Creative Thinking,* New York: Atherton Press, 141–174.

McDermott, J.F., Harrison, S.I., Schrager, J., and Wilson, P. (1965). "Social class and mental illness in children: observations of blue-collar families," *American Journal of Orthopsychiatry, 35,* 500–508.

Miller, D.R., and Swanson, G.E. (1960). *Inner Conflict and Defenses,* New York: Holt, Rinehart.

Nelson, C.M. (1971). "Techniques for screening conduct disturbed children," *Exceptional Children, 37* (7), 501–507.

Nordstrom, C., Freidenberg, E.Z., and Gold, H.A. (1967). *Society's Children: A Study of Resentiment in the Secondary School.* New York: Random House.

Penny, R.K. (1965). "Reactive curiosity and manifest anxiety in children," *Child Development, 36,* 692–702.

Phillips, E.L., Phillips, E.A., Fixen, D.L., and Wolf, M. (1973). "Achievement Place, behavior shaping works for delinquents," *Psychology Today, 7* (1), 75–79.

Pickerel, E.W. (1958). "The differential effect of manifest anxiety on test performance," *Journal of Educational Psychology, 49,* 43–46.

Pinckney, E.R. and Pinckney, C. (1965). *The Fallacy of Freud and Psychoanalysis,* Englewood Cliffs, N.J.: Prentice-Hall.

Robbins, L.N. (1966). *Deviant Children Grown Up,* Baltimore: Williams and Wilkins.

Rogers, C.R. (1942). "The criteria used in a study of mental health problems," *Education Research Bulletin,* Ohio State University Research Bureau, 2, 29–40.

Rogers, C.R. (1969). *Freedom to Learn.* Columbus, Ohio: Charles E. Merrill.

Rogers, J.M. (1971) "Drug abuse—just what the doctor ordered," *Psychology Today, 5* (September), 16, 18, 20, 24.

Salter, A. (1961). *Conditioned Reflex Therapy, The Direct Approach to the Reconstruction of Personality,* New York: Capricorn.

Schiff, J.L. (1969). "Reparenting schizophrenics," *Transactional Analysis Bulletin, 8* (31), 47–63.

Schroeder, L.B. (1965). "A study of relationships between five descriptive categories of emotional disturbance and reading and arithmetic achievement," *Exceptional Children, 32,* 111–112.

Shimota, H.E. (1964). "Reading skills in emotionally disturbed, institutionalized adolescents," *Journal of Educational Research, 58, 106–111.*

Silverman, R.E. (1954). "Anxiety and the mode of response," *Journal of Abnormal and Social Psychology, 49,* 583–592.

Smock, C.D. (1962). "The influence of psychological stress on the intolerance of ambiguity," *Journal of Abnormal and Social Psychology, 50,* 557–573.

Sobey, F. (1970). *The Nonprofessional Revolution in Mental Health,* New York: Columbia University Press.

Sprague, R.L., Barnes, K.R., and Werry, J.S. (1970). "Methylphenidate and thioridazine: learning, reaction time and classroom behavior in disturbed children," *American International Journal of Orthopsychiatry, 49,* 615–628.

Stott, D.H. (1960). "A new delinquency prediction instrument using behavioral indications," *International Journal of Social Psychiatry, 6,* 195–205.

Swift, M.S., and Spivack, G. (1969). "Achievement related classroom behavior of secondary school normal and disturbed students," *Exceptional Children, 9* (35), 677–685.

Szasz, T.S. (1961). *The Myth of Mental Illness,* New York: Hoeber.

Taylor, J.A., and Spence, K. (1952). "The relationship of anxiety to level of performance in serial learning," *Journal of Experimental Psychology, 45,* 61–64.

Ullman, L.P., and Krasner, L. (1965). "What is behavior modification?" in L.P. Ullman and L. Krasner (Eds.), *Case Studies in Behavior Modification,* New York: Holt, Rinehart, and Winston, 1–63.

Walsh, J.F., and O'Connor, J.D. (1968). "When are children disturbed?" *Elementary School Journal, 68,* 353–356.

Werry, J.S., and Quay, H. (1969). "Observing the classroom behavior of elementary children," *Exceptional Children, 35,* 461–467.

Westman, J.C., Rice, D.L., and Berman, E. (1967). "Nursery school behavior and later school adjustment," *American Journal of Orthopsychiatry, 37,* 725–731.

White, K. (1968). "Anxiety, extroversion-introversion and divergent thinking ability," *Journal of Creative Behavior, 2,* 119–127.

White, M.A. (1965). "Little red schoolhouse and little white clinic," *Teachers College Record, 66,* 188–200.

White, M.A., and Harris, M.W. (1961). "Mental illness in relation to pupil population," *The School Psychologist,* New York: Harper and Row, 119–198.

Wickman, E.K. (1928). *Childrens' Behavior and Teachers' Attitudes,* New York: Commonwealth Fund.

Yablonsky, L. (1962). *The Violent Gang,* New York: Macmillan.

Yerkes, R.M., and Dodson, J.D. (1908). "The relation of strength of stimulus to rapidity of habit formation," *Journal of Comparative and Neurological Psychology, 18,* 459–482.

Yule, W., and Rutter, M. (1968). "Educational aspects of childhood maladjustment: some epidemiological findings," *British Journal of Educational Psychology, 38,* 7–9.

Zax, M., Cowen, E.L., Rappaport, J., Beach, D.R., and Laird, J.D. (1968). "Follow-up study of children identified early as emotionally disturbed," *Journal of Consulting and Clinical Psychology, 32,* 369–374.

Zuckerman, M., Kolin, E.A., Price, L., and Zoob, I. (1964). "Development of a sensation-seeking scale," *Journal of Counseling Psychology, 28,* 477–482.

CHAPTER 2

Mike: School Phobia — Symptomatic Autism in Adolescence

WILLIAM M. EASSON

Editor's Introduction

Mike comes from an upper-middle class home with well educated, upwardly mobile parents. These socio-economic conditions usually support social, emotional, and intellectual growth, especially good physical health and school success. The fact that Mike did *not* thrive in any of these areas highlights several factors which may be missed in casual evaluations of maladjusted children.

The undiscovered hearing loss was crucial to what followed, because Mike's early learning was distorted and inconsistent. The loss was detected at 4½ years— long after the optimal period for normal speech development, and after Mike had acquired maladaptive ways of dealing with his energies, tensions, and frustrations.

Parenting was inconsistent from the start, with his mother vacillating between "smothering" and rejecting. Evidence indicates a basic rejection pattern, with subsequent guilt feelings which, in turn, temporarily aroused "smothering." This could not be sustained, however, and the thinly disguised taunts and jibes indicate the mother's basic hostility toward her son. The father is remote, not knowingly unkind, yet so immersed in his own career that he has scant time for, or real interest in the boy.

Mike's problems, therefore, have been dealt with piecemeal, usually family convenience came before the child's needs. He was intellectually bright, but terribly handicapped by the hearing loss. Disturbance was established long before he entered school, yet the piecemeal approach continued: speech therapy, hearing aid, without fundamental attention to his social or emotional problems, or change in his home situation.

The space odyssey he wrote as "Captain Mike" exemplifies a compensatory factor of imagination. The fanciful space journeys provided an escape from the pressures of his real environment. They challenged his ability, afforded a symbolic crushing of enemies, and a vent for rage without risk of self-annihilation. It was the only arena where Mike could be in control of others, as well as of himself. When anxiety built to an unbearable degree, when Mike could not remain in school because of the dizziness (which affected him only on school days!) the journal increased in violence and hostility. As Mike gained insight through his psychoanalytic sessions, "Captain Mike" grew benign towards his subjects.

With the aid of a perceptive psychiatrist, Mike is improving. Whether he will be able to fulfill his dream of becoming an astronomer is yet unclear.

There are many theoretical explanations of the etiology of autism in children. No single explanation is, as yet, universally accepted. It is interesting to note that any and all of them appear to apply to Mike, so which of them, if any, is operative in his case is speculative.

According to Rimland (1964) autism stems from a constitutional defect, an inborn dysfunction of the central nervous system which results in an impaired arousal system. However, according to Bettelheim (1967), if the arousal function were impaired, autistic children would not feel compelled to shut out incoming stimuli which, clearly, they do in a great variety of ways. Constant self-stimulation tends to blot out other stimuli from the environment. Some children close off their eyes, ears, or nostrils with their hands, others retreat to dark corners or scream furiously. Mike typed on into the night—a seemingly compulsive activity which could have served to shut out, or avoid, distracting thoughts or other unpleasant stimuli.

Bettelheim, as well as Sarvis and Garcia (1961) suggest that autism is produced by the child's *reactions* to his immediate environment. Bettelheim (1967, p. 70) states, " . . . symptomatology was not alone a reaction to generalized attitudes of parents, such as rejection, neglect, or sudden changes in mood. In addition, some specific, and for each child a different attitude or event had created in them the conviction that they were threatened by total destruction, had created the subjective feeling that they lived in an extreme situation." For Mike, such events might have been the traumatic early days in school, the dreaded school bus rides, or the even more overwhelming experience of the tonsillectomy. His mother's attitude toward him, ambivalent and shifting from moment to moment, could have conveyed threat to security and safety.

Kanner (1954) connects the development of autism to the early mother-child relationship. The child's difficulty in establishing subsequent relations with people is the outcome of early inability to relate closely and warmly with a coldly intelligent, but emotionally removed mother. Mike's mother fits Kanner's description of cold and remote.

Inability to hear, itself, diminishes the flow of stimuli from the environment. It impedes early learning experiences and establishes a model of ineffectiveness or incompetency in the handicapped individual. Mike's early propensity for creating noisy disorder around himself may have served both to reassure himself of his own existence in the vast, silent world which surrounded him, as well as to blot out of his perceptions the frightening and unintelligible stimuli which *did* break through visually, tactually, and psychologically.

MIKE AND HIS FAMILY

Mike peers searchingly into every office doorway as he strides down the hall to the waiting room. The corridor echoes to the clumping of his heavy feet. His arms swing widely at his sides, a flailing hazard to anyone passing, but Mike does not seem to notice the people around him. For the past few months Mike has been wearing a stylish, belted corduroy sports coat, but underneath he still has his dilapidated gray T-shirt and his baggy green pants, long since washed shapeless and almost colorless. Mike has grown much taller and more muscular this year. As he nears his eighteenth birthday, he is almost 6 feet, 4 inches tall and weighs over 200 pounds. He is a formidable physical specimen.

Mike has a constant quiet smile, a gentle smile, but his eyes are rarely smiling. They are deep, dark, and distant—somewhere else. His bushy sideburns make his face look thinner and longer, giving him a somber, Lincolnesque appearance. When he is thinking, he pulls these sideburns and drags the hair across to the corner of his mouth. Since summer vacation, Mike has been letting his hair grow longer; it straggles down over his collar and flops lazily over his hearing aid hidden there behind his right ear. Mike has to wear the hearing aid. He should wear two. He has been severely deaf for as long as he can remember—possibly for all his life.

A year ago, Mike's mother phoned to ask that her son "be seen in psychotherapy." She seemed to imply that she was calling in response to the recent recommendation of Mike's speech therapist. In fact, Mike's therapist was 2,000 miles away, and the recommendation had been made *two years* earlier!

When Mike and his parents were seen together, it became very obvious that the parents were seeking treatment for their son—almost any kind of treatment—because once again Mike was unable to go to school. From these initial joint evaluation interviews and from Mike's twice weekly psychotherapy sessions in the following months, the story of his development emerged.

AWARENESS OF PROBLEMS

Mike is the only son of a 45-year-old college professor. His father is pleasant and very cooperative but just cannot wait to get back to the next lecture, to see that waiting student, or to finish that urgent paper. Father is the author of several erudite texts in an engineering specialty. As he has risen in the academic profession, he and his family have moved from one college center to another every three or four years. While his father sits and smiles quietly during the interview, Mike's mother loves to talk about her son, about herself, about them and about anything. *"She just loves to talk."* As far as she is concerned, Mike is fascinating, "just fascinating —a wonderful challenge." Mike has one sister, three years older, who is attending college somewhere on the East Coast. She comes home for short one or two day visits "when she has to, when she can't get out of it," according to Mike. Even though Mike feels that his sister is "ashamed" of him, he still wears the gray T-shirts she keeps bringing.

GROWING UP WITHOUT SOLVING PROBLEMS

When Mike was born, he seemed to be "just like any other normal baby." Why he was glad and hungry and happy and irritable" and he was cuddled and everyone "just loved" this chubby, healthy little boy—or so his mother tells us. But then, when Mike was 3 months old, they had that accident. As his mother was carrying him downstairs from his bedroom, she tripped and they both fell heavily together. The parents say that Mike's skull was "fractured" at that time but Mike did not show any loss of consciousness nor were there any signs of nerve or brain damage from neurological tests. With a strident, nervous laugh and a quick wave of her hand, Mike's mother emphasizes that, of course, she had been reassured time and again that this fall did not cause Mike's deafness. Nonetheless, Mike's physical development seemed to con-

tinue normally. "Maybe he was even advanced for his age."
He walked before he was 1 year old. He was an active, in-
quisitive child, always into everything, "and you knew when
he was there" because he would rush through the house
"making noises like a siren." In and out, wailing and shouting. Mike did not seem to want friends. He was not interested
in the little boys and girls his own age. Indeed, he did not
seem to notice other children very much. As his mother
remembers, Mike did not have to bother with friends, for,
when he wanted something, he would grunt and point, and
if he did not get what he wanted, he would grunt louder or
grab. "Yes, you could hear Mike."

Before he was 2-years-old, Mike had achieved full control
of his bowels and his bladder. He seemed eager to cooperate
with his mother in learning to use the bathroom. But still he
was in and out of everything. By the time he was 3-years-old,
his parents had begun to worry because he was not talking.
They took him to the local pediatrician who examined Mike
carefully. The doctor liked the little boy. When the examination was completed, the physician was very reassuring—
Mike was absolutely healthy, "a perfect physical specimen,"
the parents should not worry—boys were often slower than
girls when it came to talking, "Mike would grow out of it."

During that next year, before Mike's fourth birthday, his
mother found that she could hardly manage him. He was
"almost uncontrollable." "He was like an uncivilized animal." He never wanted to go out and play with other children. He had no friends at all. He spent all day rushing
through his home, up and down stairs, in and out of rooms,
shrieking loudly all the time. Chaos. By evening, his mother
was exhausted with this noise and this activity. "There was
no escape."

There were times when he was quiet, "well, almost quiet,
sometimes. At least he was quieter when he was ill." Mike
began to have repeated throat infections and there was almost peace. These sore throats became so bad that at last
Mike's parents had to take him to an ear, nose, and throat
specialist. They were advised that Mike's badly infected tonsils should be removed. But there was something else. In the
course of his examination, this doctor found that Mike was
severely deaf. A neurologist who then saw Mike measured
his hearing loss at 60 decibels in each ear. This has been the
level of loss shown at each test since that time. (The engine

of a jet plane makes a noise at about the 60-decibel level). Mike's deafness was due to some defect or damage in the central part of his hearing pathways, in his brain or the nerves from the ear to the brain. Just before his fifth birthday, Mike was fitted with his first hearing aid, and his parents now had the task of teaching him first to listen and then to talk.

TREATMENT

Mike's sore throats and tonsilitis continued to recur growing worse each time. His tonsils had to be removed. Mike still can remember very clearly what happened when he went to the hospital for that operation. He could not speak. He could not hear. He did not know this strange place or those people bustling around in their white coats. His parents had left him. Then things went wrong. There was some administrative confusion. Mike was prepared for surgery, gowned in his white shirt, given his injection, but when he was taken down to the operating suite, his name was not on the operation list. For the next 8 hours, this little 5-year-old lay on his trolley outside the operating theater, half doped, half awake. The hospital staff argued about what should be done with him. Mike did not understand. He could not talk. He could not listen. At last the doctors and nurses decided to go ahead with the operation. Mike's tonsils were removed. The operation was a "success". Two days later, Mike went home and for the next two years he refused to sleep in his bedroom. He slept on a mattress placed on the floor beside his parents' bed. Every night, for months after the operation, Mike had screaming, shrieking nightmares about hospitals and white coats and needles. Mike still refuses to go to a hospital for any reason. A doctor can stitch a cut or set a fracture in his office.

Slowly and laboriously Mike's parents were teaching him to listen and to notice other people, hour after hour, over and over again. He was learning. They felt it would help him if he went to kindergarten for several hours each day to be with other children, "normal children." Mike remembers what that kindergarten was like. He remembers very vividly even now when he is almost 18, and the memories are "awful." Each morning the big school bus would come for him—that huge, noisy, frightening school bus. Off he would go in that bus where other children would be talking and doing things. But Mike did not know *what* to do. He still could not talk. He could hear sounds now but these sounds were just noises, noises without meaning, noises without purpose. Loud noises —they were painful and Mike would turn off his hearing aid; soft noises—he could hardly hear soft noises, so he could forget them. In kindergarten he would try to tell teachers and the children what he wanted. He would make his special noises, his scream, his grunt, or he would point or grab. But they did not understand either. He was just a "problem." He "did not do what he was told." He was "not obedient." He was "not polite." He did not understand all these expectations. After a week or so, Mike became such a nuisance in the kindergarten class that "they" began to punish him by shutting him away in a closet. Thirteen years later, Mike still remembers that black, silent closet, those sweaty coats hanging meanacingly up above him, that thin line of light down there teasing him from under the door. After one month, Mike refused to go to kindergarten. He kicked. He screamed. He fought. He would not go to kindergarten. He would not go on the school bus. So his first school experience lasted just four weeks, a nightmarish four weeks.

Another year went by, and Mike was seeing a speech therapist once a week. He was beginning to talk, usually one word at a time but sometimes two or three words strung together in his harsh, staccato, monotonous voice. His parents now felt that Mike was "ready to try school again." This time they decided it would be better if he went to parochial school. "The rules there are much more predictable." But the parochial school was much further away and none of Mike's neighbors went to that school; they all went to the local school which was just three or four blocks away from Mike's home. Mike had just begun to be friendly with some of the other children in the neighborhood, but now these acquaintances faded away. They went to their school. Mike went to his school.

During the initial year in the first grade in the parochial school, Mike was still "a problem." He did not do what he was told every time "but he was learning." So Mike's parents and teacher decided he should repeat the first grade "to help him communicate better." From then on everyone was pleased with Mike's progress through the first five grades in parochial school. He learned to talk in sentences. He listened to people. He did what he was told. He did not try to make friends but he followed along with the activities of his classmates. "He seemed to be happy." Now and then there were difficulties at school when Mike was "impulsive." Sometimes he had a "tantrum" when he was frustrated or upset; he would rush around shouting and screaming but then "he soon would cool off." Everything seemed to be going quite well so Mike's parents were really surprised when his speech therapist telephoned one day to suggest that he should be moved to a fifth grade class in public school "because he was too repressed."

"Too repressed?" The parents just could not see what the speech therapist was talking about—but then the family was getting ready to move again. Mike's father was transferring to a better position, so the parents took the opportunity of this move to place him in a fifth grade class in a public school in his new city.

Mike no longer had to wear a formal white shirt and tie (and he has refused to wear a shirt or tie since!) He found his new classmates much more "relaxed"; they were active and energetic too. They did not tease him, even though they found his speech difficult to understand. Mike had to wear braces on his teeth, so his words were even more slurred and indistinct. The braces were on for two years. "But things were getting better" and Mike became friends with another boy his age.

Together the young adolescents roamed the streets and explored the countryside outside the small city. Mike's parents felt that he was really happy, really a member of his peer group, "really doing well"—and Mike thought that he was doing well. He had ways, now, to "blow off steam." When he was frustrated, he no longer had to sit quiet and still in the classroom; he could go down to the gymnasium and beat out his energy on a ball. When he was upset, he could get away and work out his rage by cycling furiously round and round the school grounds.

All these years, Mike's mother had been "living for him" —and his mother says this over and over—but Mike was finding that his mother's constant concern "bugged" him. She "got" to him and she seemed to be teasing him, "needling" him, "getting under his skin." When mother laughed at his fury, and told him not to be "crazy," Mike would become almost helpless with futile rage. His mother seemed to enjoy taunting him by saying that he was "stupid," a "moron," a "fool." These words rankled deeply, but mother told him she was "only joking."

In school, Mike continued to have B, C, and D grades. According to his school reports he was "an average student." His highest grades, sometimes even A's, were in science. He excelled in astronomy, but he felt that "no one seemed to be interested in that." His seventh grade teacher was amused when Mike told her that he was a "genius" and intended to be an astronomer; his psychological tests always placed him in the average intelligence range; though his subtest scores did show a wide scatter.

During seventh grade, Mike had started to grow quite rapidly. Now he was a head taller than the other boys in his class, though they were better coordinated than he was. They teased him about his size and his awkwardness. He could not hide. He could not escape. His mother says that Mike "seemed to stay in sixth grade while his friends were growing up." So, in an effort to "push him socially," Mike's parents sent him to summer camp during vacation time between seventh and eighth grade. Another nightmare. For Mike this was a "concentration camp." He did not know what to do in a camp.

Even with a hearing aid on each ear, Mike cannot detect differences in the tone of speech or in the quality of noises. Everything he hears is in a relative monotone, so he finds it very difficult to distinguish different speakers in a group or in a noisy setting. He must see where the sounds come from in order to locate the source. When it is dark, Mike cannot tell where sounds originate.

Camp was impossible. Mike developed a steady, pounding headache which kept him in bed in his cabin. In spite of all the coaxing, teasing, and threats, Mike stayed there in bed. After one miserable week, Mike's parents came and took him home. His headache cleared, at least for that time.

In the eighth grade, "things started to get worse," *much worse*. Mike began to find that he and the other adolescents in his class "really did not speak the same language." The other teenagers wanted to be part of a gang or a group, Mike wanted to be left alone. His classmates were excited about team sports and games, Mike preferred to play by himself, a six foot tall, 14-year-old, and not on the basketball team! His teenage friends were becoming interested in girls, but Mike did not want to be concerned with "that," whatever "that" was.

More and more Mike was keeping to himself and "thinking his own thoughts." He was going back to his "old language," to what he called his "ESP". Mike has always been able to "read" people. He can feel what they are thinking before they put their thoughts into words. He can "sense their vibrations." He reads their self-confidence in the way they hold their shoulders and in the depth of their breathing. He reads their happiness and their security in the firmness of their walk. He reads the assuredness of their eyes. When the other person's eyes *look* hatred and contempt, but their voice speaks love and friendship, Mike believes the more basic message of the eyes. When their words say comfort and security to him, but their hand muscles are limp and uncertain, Mike accepts the communication of the hand. When he sees and feels the shoulders hunch in suspicion and menace, Mike reacts to the shoulder message, even though the individual speaks words of peace and acceptance.

As his few friends drifted away, Mike gradually pulled back into his inner world. He found his happiness in this private world of imagination with his own private friends. Mike thought, planned, and dreamed about all the things that were happening out in the universe, among the stars, swirling there between nebulae. In his thoughts, Mike was there, way out there, the *real* Mike, the Commander of the Fleet, hurtling from galaxy to galaxy. As the pressures on Earth increased—in school, at home—Mike spent more time out there in his fantasy spaceship, driving on to Sirius.

Toward the end of the eighth grade, Mike was out of school for two periods of six weeks due to "dizziness." He had many different medical and neurological examinations, but no one could find any definite cause for his dizziness. Mike just could not get up from bed in the morning because he was so dizzy. He saw specialist after specialist. As Mike looks back now, he thinks the dizziness occurred more often in the mornings, was worse Monday through Friday, and somehow was not nearly as bad on weekends. When he was upset or excited, and especially when he was angry, the dizziness would develop. He would go to bed and the dizziness would gradually clear "after a few hours." Usually by the evening his dizziness had gone. During the summer months between the eighth and ninth grades, Mike was happy and well. His dizziness was "cured." He played by himself in the corner of his backyard where he was planning his spaceship.

Next fall, Mike was only two weeks into ninth grade when the dizziness returned so severely that he could not go to school. Twice again, just before Christmas, he tried to return to school, but each time he could stay only one day in class. His dizziness made it impossible to stay in school. At home he continued to work with his school books and, when he took the regular class examination, his grades were above the class average. His mother who had been "amusing herself" by taking classes in Divinity School, decided she should stay at home to look after Mike "because he could not do without me." She "just had to live her life for him" but, in one interview, Mike's mother described how she was always doing something for him "unless I could escape"; after this statement, mother laughed that her "oral diarrhea" had just "run away" from her at that moment.

Even at home, Mike's tension periodically mounted to the point where he had to cycle around the block for hours in order to "unwind." During one of these cycling marathons, Mike ran over a brick, was thrown from his bicycle and grazed his legs badly. In spite of his mother's careful attention, the skin over both knees became severely infected. Mike was feverish, shivery, and in constant pain. He could hardly move. He spent his day sitting stiffly on a wooden chair in front of a silent television set, unable to eat, unable to move, unable to watch. Yet he refused to go to the hospital, even to the out-patient department. Mike "went out of his mind with fear" at that idea, according to both Mike and his mother. Eventually his knees became so swollen and painful and his conditions so toxic that his parents forcibly took him to the hospital out-patient clinic where they sat "holding him down." Mike tells how he waited there, quivering with a nameless panic, dreading that "they" would cut off his legs or "do something awful." He watched the smiling nurses and he knew that they were laughing at him. He looked at the other teenage patients and he hated them "because they were phony." Eventually Mike's knees healed with the treatment he received, and he was able to be up and doing again. He thinks he "nearly went out of his mind" during those weeks when he had to sit immobile and think, think, think.

Once again, Mike's father was transferring to another college where, this time, he would be a full professor. The family moved and Mike started in another public school, once more at the ninth grade level. In this new school, Mike "resolved to do well." He knew he had to do well. He knew he must graduate from high school so that he could go to college to be an astronomer. He tried very hard to stay in school, but gradually school became intolerable. In the crossfire of questions and discussions between student and teacher in the classroom, Mike never knew who was speaking or where the sound would come from next. He never fully understood what was being said or whether he was being questioned. When the teacher looked and spoke in his direction, Mike never was quite sure if *he* was being asked, or whether it was the boy beside him, or the girl just behind, or even that boy over there. When he tried to speak, his speech was slow and awkward. When he was worried, he hesitated even more over his words, and the other students laughed and the teacher smiled. When he walked along the school hallway with the other members of his class, he was six inches taller than they were. Everyone looked at him. Everyone watched him. Then he would "become tense" and stumble, and they would laugh. He felt they were just waiting to tease him again. They would hurt him—he knew they would. He watched them, the teachers, the other teenagers. He read them. He read the way they looked at him. He read the way they sat in the classroom and out on the grass. He read the way they dressed. He read the way they walked. He could feel what they were thinking, and he knew it all before they said it. His constant tension grew worse. He spent long evenings and well into the night thinking about Commander Mike up there on his spaceship, zooming onward at several times the speed of light, onward and away, away. Mike started to keep a ship's record of his flights between the galaxies, and every night he typed out the day's flight log, typing, one finger at a time, typing through the night. His parents lay awake listening to the beat-beat of the typewriter—but they knew he was at least typing English composition and learning spelling.

Quite suddenly Mike's dizziness started to come back. There was no special reason at school why he should feel worse. Mike said "things were awful, but they were always awful then." In the last week before the Christmas vacation, Mike was so dizzy in school that he could hardly stand. He just "sat it out" in the classroom, waiting for the hours to pass, waiting until he could get home to his dreams of space travel and space wars between the planets. The chatter and the bustle of the classroom swirled around him. He said nothing. He sat quiet. He did not know what was happening but he sat there. On the first school day after Christmas vacation, Mike's dizziness was so bad that he could not go to school. He could hardly get out of bed to eat breakfast and, you know, "he eats like a horse, anytime."

It was *that afternoon* that Mike's mother phoned to ask for psychiatric treatment. Mike and the psychiatrist started meeting for two sessions each week, initially as part of his evaluation, but eventually in an ongoing treatment process.

At first Mike could remember very little about what had happened to him in the past. He sat stiffly in his chair and talked in a dull, pounding monotone about what he had done that day—and what he was usually doing was writing his book. He was writing about Commander Mike out there between the planets, leading his Space Armada to conquer the universe. Week after week Mike described his book. The battles. The annihilation. The planets exploding. The nations devastated. The speeding, invulnerable spaceship roaming the universe, unchallenged. Commander Mike, young, virile, cold, merciless, intent on conquest. Commander Mike cared for no one. He destroyed continents and planets at whim. His order was absolute. Men died, cities disintegrated, nations atomized—if they displeased Commander Mike.

All the time Mike was talking about his book, he was reading the psychiatrist carefully. He was looking into the doctor's eyes, watching the movement of his face, sensing the meaning of his posture. While they talked about the book, Mike and the doctor also started to talk to each other in an unspoken language. The psychiatrist also read Mike's eyes, Mike's face, Mike's posture and, without comment, began to react to these non-verbal messages. Mike started to respond to this communication. Gradually the pattern of Mike's book began to change. Commander Mike, far out in space, speeding between the stars, began to be more sensitive to other people. Sometimes he was merciful and did not raze a city; sometimes he forgave and spared the conquered planet. Slowly, over the months, the theme of Mike's book changed. The slaughter, the explosiveness, the furious racing from galaxy to galaxy so many thousand light years away—the tumult decreased until there came a chapter in this book when Commander Mike did not destroy at all. It was at about this time that the psychiatrist gently began to interpret what Mike was saying in his book and started to apply the message of the book to what Mike was feeling and thinking on this planet Earth. Mike and the doctor began to talk about Mike's inner explosiveness, his fury, his fierce drive, his hunger, and, now and then, about his isolation, his absolute aloneness, his own private, personal universe.

Mike thought about going back to school but, as he started to make plans to return, his book began to tell about total obliteration, overwhelming destruction and absolute, uncontrolled violence. When Mike, his psychiatrist, and his parents decided that he should be tutored at home rather than return to public school, peace came once more to Mike's book. Commander Mike out there in furthest space became merciful and gentle again.

Mike was assigned three homebound schoolteachers to teach him English, American history, and mathematics. These teachers like Mike and, to his dismay, he is finding that he likes them, "well, *almost* likes them." He has begun to share his book with his new teachers. His mathematics instructor works with him in computing travel speeds between the planets; his history teacher spends much time charting the history of our planet until this age of man; his English teacher accepts the weekly chapter he produces as a creative writing project.

Mike has started to emerge again from his house. When he is tense or frustrated, he runs around the neighborhood, often late at night, or he cycles several miles out into the country. His father put up a basketball net outside the garage and Mike spends long hours, often in rain or in snow, throwing a ball through the hoop—"a great way to work out tension, Doc."

Mike is not back in school. He will not go near the school buildings, not even to see the school basketball team. Probably he never will return to high school. He is finishing tenth grade now and most likely will work toward high school graduation with his homebound teachers. He still talks about going to college, to major in astronomy. He thinks there will be "less pressure" in college, and he feels that he can "escape" more easily from a college class. He has what he calls "a few acquaintances," mostly neighbor boys his own age, with whom he "throws a basketball" or "kicks a football." That is all he wants from them. He does not try to know these teenagers. He certainly does not wish *them* to know *him*. Why should he be concerned about them? They are not interested in astronomy. They "fuss too much" about clothes and girls and cars, and "these things" bore Mike.

Mike's parents find that he is much easier to "tolerate." He does not run about the house all the time now. "It has been months since he had an explosion." He "cooperates" with his mother and father. They do not have "to watch him." Yes, mother is planning to go back to college again. She may take psychology courses this time. His father is writing another book.

Mike can discuss his deafness now. He talks about the private languages he uses, the way he reads people. He says he is "different" and he feels he will always be different. He lives in a different world, the world of a child who has grown up deaf, who first learned to think and feel, and later, *only later,* learned to listen and to talk.

References

Bettelheim, B. (1967). *The Empty Fortress,* New York, The Free Press.
Kanner, L. (1954). "To what extent is early infantile autism determined by constitutional inadequacy?" *Proceedings of the Association for Research on Nervous and Mental Disease, 33,* 378–385.
Rimland, B. (1964). *Infantile Autism,* New York: Appleton.
Sarvis, M. S. and Garcia, P. (1961). "Etiological variables in autism," *Psychiatry, 24,* 307–317.

Related Reading

Autism

Benda, C. E. (1960) "Childhood Schizophrenia, autism and Heller's Disease." P. W. Bowman and H. V. Mautner (Eds.), *Mental Retardation.*
Eisenberg, L. (1956). "The autistic child in adolescence," *American Journal of Psychiatry, 112,* 607–612.
Eveloff, H.H. (1960). "The autistic child," *Archives of General Psychiatry, 3,* 66–81.
Rutter, M. (1968). "Concepts of autism: a review of research," *Journal of Child Psychology and Psychiatry, 9,* 1–25.
Schain, R.J., and Yannet, H. (1960). "Infantile autism—an analysis of 50 cases," *Journal of Pediatrics, 57,* (4), 560–567.

Emotional Handicaps and the Deaf

Charlton, B. (1970). "A group treatment approach to multiple problem behaviors of autistic children," *Exceptional Children, 36,* 765–770.

Myklebust, H. (1963). "Psychological and psychiatric implications of deafness," *Archives of Otolarynogology, 78,* 790–793.

Rainer, J.D., Altshuler, K.Z., and Kallman, F.J. (Eds.) (1963). *Family and Mental Health Problems in a Deaf Population,* New York: Department of Medical Genetics, N.Y. State Psychiatric Institute, Columbia University.

Shears, L.M., and Jensema, C.J. (1969). "Social acceptability of anomolous persons," *Exceptional Children, 36,* 91–96.

Learning Disabilities and the Deaf

McConnell, F., and Ward, P. (Eds.) (1967). *Deafness in Childhood,* Nashville: Vanderbilt University Press.

Withrow, F.B. (1968). "Immediate memory span of deaf and normally hearing children," *Exceptional Children, 35,* 33–41.

School Phobia

Blackham, G.J. (1967). The *Deviant Child in the Classroom,* Belmont, Calif.: Wadsworth, (1962). 165–171.

Kahn, J.H., and Nursten, J.P. (1962). "School refusal: a comprehensive review of school phobia and other failures of school attendance," *American Journal of Orthopsychiatry, 32,* 707–718.

Kessler, J.W. (1966). *Psychopathology of Childhood,* Englewood Cliffs, N.J.: Prentice-Hall, 238–243.

Levison, B. (1962) "Understanding the child with school phobia," *Exceptional Children, 28,* 393–397.

CHAPTER 3

Jean: A Case of
Pseudo-Retardation

D. H. STOTT

Editor's Introduction

If mental retardation indicates a combination of subaverage intellectual functioning and impaired adaptive behavior, pseudoretardation implies a counterfeit condition in which "true" retardation is not present. Obviously, it would be impossible for an individual to feign *giftedness* if, in fact, he lacked the requisite intellectual qualities. However, a person can readily function at a *lower* level than that of which he is potentially capable. If a young child's actual capabilities never have been displayed, and if his needs are tolerably well satisfied when he responds to his environment in a "retarded" way, then he may adopt an inferior style. The classification of pseudoretardation only can be applied *after the fact,* that is, after the individual has shown himself *not* to be retarded.

This counterfeit, like others, tends to have identifiable, albeit subtle, flaws. Stott, in observing the regressed behavior of 4-year-old Jean "lying on the floor in a pose of pity-exciting misery" noted that Jean's eyes followed the hovering and solicitous adults, gauging their reactions to her behavior. He was also cued because Jean took the lead while playing with her brother. Her effective response to behavior modification gives validity to the view that retarded behavior had been preferred *because it paid off.* When the contingencies were reordered, Jean's "retardation" faded.

As in the Morse and Lockett study (chapter 8), this case illustrates careful, individualized handling of a troubled child. The situation was assessed and reassessed. Materials were unique, challenging, expertly used, and presented in appropriate sequence. Continued follow-through resulted in sequential environmental settings appropriate to the child's progress. At all stages, Jean was considered an individual with a unique problem.

Jean clearly illustrates Stott's thesis that a troubled child has become the focus of a constellation of difficulties, each of which has made subtle changes in the nervous system, and ultimately in total development and behavior. Characteristically, there were family disruptions as well as physical and mental health problems during pregnancy. The birth itself was complicated, and Jean was seriously ill during her first week of life. Subsequently, all developmental expectations were achieved late. Dependency was prolonged and exploited to the extent that Jean was deriving more satisfactions from being "helpless" and "retarded" than from becoming increasingly independent and normal in functioning.

Stott's study suggests that some apparent retardates may, in fact, simply be reflecting a series of small misfortunes which, as an aggregate, impede the emergence of normal behavior. The need for very careful observation, assessment, and then individualized retraining is imperative.

JEAN

The subject of this report is a 4-year-old girl who assumed the role of retardate as a way of life, was diagnosed as such and placed in a nursery for the retarded. Through a rehabilitation program she was persuaded to abandon this role and to function at a normal level of mental ability. Experience with retarded children suggests that such cases are not uncommon, even though there are a variety of reasons for their choice of the retardate's role. The condition of pseudoretardation may thus remain undiagnosed, so that the child continues to be treated as a retardate, the evidence to the contrary is unseen because it is too dissonant with our conceptions and with the accepted role.

We cannot proceed further without defining our terms. The definition of mental deficiency given by the *Manual of the American Association on Mental Deficiency* (Heber, 1959) has been criticized (Garfield and Wittson, 1960; Halpern, 1970) for laying chief stress upon current functioning. Social adjustment, broadly conceived, is one of the criteria for mental deficiency. Whereas it is recognized that failure thereof may result from intellectual deficit, no attempt is made to differentiate between intrinsic *inability* to meet the requirements of an independent life due to cognitive impairment and *malfunctioning* which is due to motivational aberration. It is upon this distinction that the concept of pseudoretardation rests. In his current functioning, the pseudoretardate is indeed mentally retarded, but he may not be "truly" retarded in the cognitive sense, as defined below, in that, once the motivational aberration is removed, he may be able to function at a normal intellectual level.

What makes us suspect that in some cases the child is not truly retarded is his apparent ability to function at a normal level at certain times or in some areas. This is the basic concept underlying Benton's pseudofeeblemindedness or psychogenic mental deficiency (1962). He points out that among normal people a "subject matter disability, as in mathematics or literature" is accepted without question. In other words, a normal person is permitted to be "retarded" in some areas. If, however, the areas of retardation reach a certain size or impinge upon functions that traditionally are associated with "low intelligence," the person is classifed as retarded.

The detection of pseudoretardation requires, in consequence, the systematic study and recording of an individual's functioning in a variety of situations over a period of time. The observed behaviors then can be classified as, on the one hand, demonstrating ability to function at a level of complexity which enables the individual to operate effectively and to achieve his goals or, on the other hand, inability to cope with situations at such a level. If there is an underlying consistency in this inconsistency of function we may begin to suspect pseudoretardation.

The criterion of complexity enables us to differentiate between cognitive (true?) retardation and socially maladaptive behavior. In the case to be described, the child operated at a high level of complexity in order to maintain a socially maladaptive, and indeed a "retarded" role. Normally such a role would be judged highly detrimental to the child's best interests but, in fact, she was achieving an effective manipulation of her environment.

Benton likewise suggests that situational retardation, that is, pseudofeeblemindedness, may arise from motivational factors, examples of aversive conditioning by early unpleasant or traumatic experiences. Whereas the development of these "emotional blocks" cannot be denied, and indeed may be seen as important pseudoadjustments, other authors (Chess, 1967, 1968) have drawn attention to primary handicaps of temperament, which would appear to be congenital. Nevertheless, in using the word "temperament" we have to beware of falling into the trap of postulating yet another mystical "essence"—with the presumption of permanency— against which Hunt (1961) warns in the concept of "intelligence." Empirically defined, a person's temperament represents expectations about his behavior which have arisen because of his tendency to behave in more or less consistent ways in typical life-situations. It leaves open the reasons for the establishment of such behavioral regularities.

The concept of temperament—or the adoption of consistent situational roles—clarifies another source of confusion in the diagnosis of mental retardation which centers around the concept of a motivational or "emotional" factor. These terms are variously and loosely used. In the present discussion the term "emotional," although popular, is avoided as being inaccurate. "Motivation" is defined as comprising the factors which determine the individual's choice of goals, more precisely, the types of relationships which the agent seeks to establish between himself and his world (Nissen, 1958). What looks at first sight like extremely ineffective functioning may, in the light of his chosen goals, be highly effective and "intelligent." He may decide to avoid coping with certain situations altogether, either because they are deemed unrewarding or because other goals demand non-coping. In the case of our girl, maintenance of her dependency role required consistent noncoping in everyday situations, above all, those in which an adult demanded some achievement. Reduced to ultimate objectivity, the motivational variable is a matter of whether behaviors of a certain class occur or not. This applies also to cognitive processes. *De facto* mental retardation may arise either because such processes are grossly impaired, or because they do not occur (or a combination of both). It is suspected that much mental retardation results from non-use of cognitive functions, that is to say, is of motivational origin. Since the efficiency of the cognitive processes comes in question only when they occur, the motivational factor can be the overriding one. A formal intelligence test score does not distinguish between motivational and cognitive impairment. Failure on an item—hence the IQ as a whole—may be due either to the subject's inability to operate at the requisite level of complexity or to a failure to initiate the cognitive processes. In the present case-study the apparent retardation was entirely of the latter sort. Once the cognitive processes were brought into play they were seen to be of normal quality.

It is tempting to accept the possibility of motivational retardation as an exceptional phenomenon while retaining the convenient traditional diagnosis in terms of "mental level." However, experience with many cases in a remedial clinic to which children were referred from primary departments of schools as slow learners led us to the view that practically all such cases are of motivational origin, without significant impairment of the cognitive proceeses as such. When it comes to the category of the "trainable retarded," with a traditional IQ ceiling of 50–55, it is apparent that significant cognitive impairment exists in many, even though at a lesser level than is supposed. On the other hand, the use of a diagnostic system based upon the observation and recording of everyday and learning behavior (Stott, 1971b) reveals that a considerable minority even of the "trainable retarded" may be termperamentally (motivationally) rather than cognitively impaired.

If, as argued above, occurrence or nonoccurrence of a process is more fundamental than its quality when it does occur, the first step in the diagnosis of retardation should be the assessment of the motivational variable. Such an approach requires the means of identifying and classifying temperamental factors in learning disability. Mention can be made only of one type of temperamental impairment as being relevant to the discussion of the case. Chess recognizes it in her "slow-to-warm-up" type of child. Sontag (1962) stressed its aspect of social apprehensiveness. The writer and his collaborators (Stott and Sykes, 1971; Stott, 1971c) have named it "unforthcomingness." The symptoms are a withdrawal from any situation, social or material, which contains an element of strangeness, uncertaintly, or supposed difficulty. Murphy (1962) emphasizes the essential normality of feelings of this sort, but describes a very convincing case of a little girl who consciously decides to master her fears of thunder and of the doctor's and dentist's offices. What seems to be lacking in the unforthcoming child is not so much an abnormal fearfulness as a lack of the determination to master normal fears. In the writer's view, this may be conceptualized as an impairment of effectiveness-motivation (1961) or, in White's (1959) terminology, of the urge towards competence. It is not feelings of apprehensiveness which are diagnostically important so much as the actual withdrawal from or avoidance of situations with which the normal child, even with some hesitation, decides to cope.

Just before her fourth birthday, Jean, the subject of the present case-study, was admitted to a nursery for mentally retarded on the recommendation of a psychologist and a public health nurse. No intelligence test was given because she was patently untestable. To all appearances she was severely retarded, and her extreme helplessness was the cause of considerable concern to the nursery director. Any attempt to bring her into an activity was met by turning away, lying on the floor, and a pose of pity-exciting misery. This style of behavior was reinforced by the good-hearted but untrained helpers, who would pick her up and nurse her patiently whenever she adopted it, with the result that the greater part of her time in the nursery was spent in someone's arms. She never mixed with other children or played with the available toys.

Jean became the subject of clinical study at the age of 4½. Interviewed at this time, the mother reported somewhat similar lethargy and miserableness in behavior at home, but added that she indulged in temper tantrums followed by sulking when she could not get her own way. However, she played well on the whole with her brother one year younger than herself, and, most surprisingly, usually took the lead.

The family consisted of five children ranging from 13 to 3 years, all of whom were stable and functioning well except Jean, the fourth. The parents were sensible and stable, and led a well-organized middle-class life. The mother did not go out to work, but was taking extension courses at the university. She had the warm, protective maternal style found in the Mediterranean and many other traditional cultures. She accepted the fact that Jean was retarded and reinforced her dependence strategy in much the same way as did nursery helpers.

Observed from behind a one-way mirror in the nursery, Jean's general manner certainly gave the appearance of severe retardation. There was, however, one telltale contradiction. Even when lying inert on the floor she would be following one adult or another with her eyes, presumably to gauge the effects of her behavior.

The first therapeutic objective was to halt the reinforcement of Jean's dependence strategy. A meeting was held with the nursery helpers at which it was pointed out how she was able to command constant attention, and in fact very effectively controlled their behavior. They were led to see that so long as she was allowed to enjoy this form of fulfillment she would not progress, and there would be no means of finding out whether she was retarded or not. Very specific guidance was given to them never to pick her up when she collapsed whimpering on the floor, and if she did not care to participate in the musical and other social activities she was simply to be ignored. With one or two lapses the helpers faithfully carried out this program.

A similar explanation and similar counseling were given to the mother. It was not anticipated that she would be able to carry out such a radical change of attitude without further guidance, but throughout the treatment she showed the most commendable determination to cooperate.

The behavior-modification treatment in the nursery began to show good results within a matter of days. Bored with lying unattended on the floor, Jean made her way over to the toy corner and occupied herself with the toys. Within a short while she began to interact with other children, utilizing the same pattern of interaction as with her younger brother.

At this stage she was included in a group of about her own age who were beginning the Flying Start Learning-to-Learn Program (Stott, 1971a). This consists of a programmed series of puzzles and other play-activities for kindergarten and pre-kindergarten children, so designed that success can be achieved only if the requisite perceptual and cognitive processes are brought into play. It thus represents an adaptation of the principles of behavior-modification in the direction not of reducing undesirable but of producing desirable behavior. The types of activity correspond to the kinds of effect which a child naturally seeks to achieve in order to be effective (White, 1959; Stott, 1961) and thus are spontaneously motivating. Since occurrence of cognitive processes is consistently reinforced, the Program serves to correct those problem-solving strategies which for one reason or another (avoidance, impulsivity, etc.) result in nonoccurrence.

The first item requires merely that the child join the two halves of a boldly drawn picture. In order to preclude mere trial-and-error fitting and to reinforce attention and cognitive rehearsal, the picture is divided by a straight rather than by a curved cut such as usually found in play-materials for the retarded. On being presented with this task Jean showed no sign of comprehending what was expected of her. Her lack of response could easily have resulted in failure on an intelligence test. However, despite her moping she followed closely with her eyes the successful efforts of the other three children. She resisted all cajoling to participate. Then the therapist, in the course of handing out fresh pieces to the others, laid in front of her the two halves of a picture only a short distance apart. He made no comment and paid no further attention to her. The other children joined their halves and were duly praised. Jean, forgetting momentarily her role of nonparticipant, could not resist pushing the two halves of her picture together. Attention was drawn to her accomplishment and she was fulsomely praised. In the next round another picture was placed in front of her with the halves similarly almost joined, and again without any injunction to participate. She put them together quickly this time. It was obvious that they presented her with no perceptual or other mechanical difficulty. Finally each half was presented to her separately, and she completed the picture straightaway.

The next week she completed the same picture cut into quarters. Progressively, also, she began playing happily with

Fig. 1. Showing the happy, active life-style that Jean (right) progressively adopted. She is posting letters in the Mail Box game of the *Flying Start Learning-to-Learn Kit.*

other children and began experimenting in the use of an active, initiative-taking life-style. With little hesitation she embarked upon the next of the "Flying Start" tasks, which consisted of mailing small cards, each bearing a letter, into "mailboxes" bearing similar letters (see Fig. 1). She concentrated on this activity with what the research assistant described as "super-focus." At the same time, as would be expected of a normal child, she became bored with the picture completion.

A week later she was beginning to become more assertive and to exploit her new life-style to the point of being described as disruptive. She was reported as frequently smiling, and even laughing heartily, and showing an "exaggerated independence." In group activities she became competitive, trying to build a "biggie, biggie, biggie tower." The research assistant noted that "she does not lack competence in meddlesome activity."

The next week she had a partial relapse. The volunteer

who had ministered to her all too affectionately returned after several weeks off duty and there was not time to brief her adequately in the new therapeutic strategy. Her presence evidently reactivated Jean's desire for control through dependence. She refused to answer her name in the circle. Half her time during the play activities she spent watching the movements of her favorite volunteer. Yet, to quote from the nursery director's daily notes, "participation and enjoyment amounted to a much greater part of the morning than non-participation and unhappiness." Notably, she did excellently at the mailboxes.

Four days later she definitely opted for the outgoing, participating style as evidently bringing greater rewards. She sang a verse of a song by herself in the circle, became very affable and, after correctly identifying the numbers 1 to 10 became quite "hyper" at her accomplishment. The only contretemps was when she cried at having to lie on a mat alone instead of having a volunteer beside her, but she stopped after two minutes of being ignored. During this period she began to wet her pants but desisted when she was made to visit the bathroom every hour.

At this time, some two months after the beginning of the treatment, her behavior was rated on the Effectiveness-Motivation Scale (Stott and Sharp, 1968). Descriptions of typical levels of effectiveness are scored from 0 to 4 in 11 areas of functioning, such as Building, Creative Play, Make-Believe Play, Appeal to Novelty, Helping Others, Reactions to Strangers. She scored 30, which is half a standard deviation above the mean of 24 for a normal nursery-school sample. This result showed that, contrary to first appearances, she could not be rated as in any way an unforthcoming child. Her occasional reluctance to tackle new tasks stemmed, in so far as it was not normal, rather from her harking back to a dependence/incompetence strategy.

A week later the nursery director was writing of Jean, "Behavior practically normal, very happy playing in a group with small cars. The quarter cards and the mailboxes seem too easy for her when she is in a cooperative mood." The next day she had her "best day ever" in the swimming baths, not only undressing and dressing herself but attempting to help dress the volunteer. She jumped into the pool willingly and bobbed her head under the water, which is anything but characteristic of a temperamentally apprehensive child.

During the following weeks she maintained her happy, outgoing participating style with only slight lapses. She did not mind which volunteer worked with her, and she helped to organize the children for various games and songs. On arrival she ran off from her mother eagerly in order to show how well she was doing at her activities. She made no attempt to interrupt her mother's socializing at the end of the sessions but busied herself by putting on her own coat, hat, and boots. This transformation in her behavior and level of mental functioning had taken not quite three months. During the next few weeks it was apparent that Jean was out of place and had reached the limit of her progress in the retarded nursery. Also, since she was just turned 5, it was important to prepare her for entry to a normal kindergarten. It was therefore decided to introduce her to the kindergarten group at the *Centre for Educational Disabilities,* composed of children referred as slow learners but, like Jean, showing for the most part faulty styles of learning behavior rather than poor ability.

On her first visit to the Centre she was brought by a nursery volunteer who had been firm with her, and she settled down well to the learning activities. By now she could do the six-piece puzzles and worked with a good, thoughtful strategy. However, she decided to test her earlier strategy of moodiness and fretting on the Centre volunteer, and whined for her mother, whom she knew would be fetching her. On subsequent visits she made sporadic, albeit successful efforts with the learning materials but continued to behave in a petulant way. The crisis came when we asked the mother to leave her at the Centre and return to fetch her at the end of the session. This she was prepared to do, but Jean clung to her, crying, and the mother was in a helpless state of conflict between her old and new methods of handling the child. She was told, in defiance of orthodox therapeutic practice, to give Jean a smack on the bottom, send her into the playroom and then leave herself. She administered the smack in a half-hearted way and one of the Centre staff pulled Jean screaming into the playroom. This tactic was used in the confidence that Jean suffered from no genuine apprehensions but was making a last desperate effort to maintain an unprogressive strategy of control. Once in the room she stood against one of the playhouses whimpering, but characteristically watching the activities of the other children. After a minute or two she gave up the whimpering and just stood, sporadically making indecisive movements to join them. After just over five minutes a kindergarten girl came up to her and said, "Do you want to come and play or stand there crying?" When the other child took her by the hand Jean followed and after a few minutes, she participated in the cutting of paper shapes. During the subsequent learning-activity sessions she made further attempts to manipulate the teacher by pouting, but when she saw this had no effect became friendly and talkative. She mentioned her wish to have yellow shoes to match her yellow dress (she could distinguish all the basic colors). By now she had reached the 8-piece animal puzzles, could do them surprisingly quickly, and was delighted with her success.

On subsequent visits the same alternation of strategies persisted, but with the dependent, moody one becoming progressively less frequent. She could quickly see when the "game was up." One might say that she was now behaving like any rather spoiled 4-year-old.

Intellectually she made great strides. She needed very little encouragement to do the final set of animal puzzles of ten pieces, and they presented no difficulty to her. She overcame her resistance to the matchers game and eventually completed the first ten series. This item of the *Flying Start Program* demands not only good problem-solving strategies but the use of fairly complex cognitive processes. For example, a picture of a pirate has to be matched from among a row of six which contain systematic variants (see Fig. 2). In three of the pictures, the pirate wears a hat, in three he is bareheaded. The distinction has to be held in mind (cognitively "stored") while the feet are examined. In two pictures the pirates have feet intact, two have a wooden peg in lieu of the right leg and two a wooden peg in lieu of the left. Thus the child has to withhold his choice until he has made two successive discriminations, and for four out of six the additional one of sidedness.

It is part of the compensatory program for slow-learning kindergarten children in the above Centre to help them attain the elementary concepts of quantity and numeration, and also the phonic principle that letters represent sounds. Jean had already mastered the idea of counting, and played the Number Games with success and enthusiasm. She provided us with our biggest surprise by her rapid mastery of

Fig. 2.   The Matchers Game in the *Flying Start Learning-to-Learn Kit*.

The card in front has to be matched against one of the six in

the row, involving discrimination by three criteria.

phonic encoding. The method used is based on the little recognized fact that the learner must associate the letter-symbol not with a separately pronounced "sound" but with the phoneme as actually pronounced in the word context. This method of teaching the phonic basis of reading, although more realistic and efficient, means that the child has to learn to listen to words and to associate their various beginning sounds with letters. Since, at the age of five years, very few children know what is meant by a "word", let alone a "sound" (Downing, 1970), the associational task requires something more than simple paired-associate learning. By means of the Giant Touch Cards of the *Programmed Reading Kit* (Stott, 1962) the process is programmed into the stages, first of learning to listen to initial sounds, second of noting the shapes of the letters, and third of associating initial sound with letter. In the course of a game of some 15 minutes it is usual to teach a group of children only four such associations. In her first session, Jean learned all nine of the first set, showing no lack of confidence or hesitation, and demanded to be allowed to go on to the next set of 10. She got all these correct except the "k" (having previously had the same sound for "c").

If, at the end of her two months in the Centre's kindergarten group, she still had any temperamental handicap, it was that she never became a compliant child. She wanted to control her own world and to follow her own motivations. She would agree to do the things that pleased her, or, when pushed, what was necessary to assure being allowed later to do what she wished. If she rejected one learning activity it was usually because she preferred another. She had a wide range of strategies, such as feigning fatigue, or wanting to go the washroom, and continually appraised her chances of having her own way. One might attribute this defect, if that it be, to her high effectiveness-motivation combined with a lack of social conditioning within the permissive atmosphere of her home. Her behavior resembled that of an intelligent younger child.

Two weeks before the end of her time at the Centre, Jean was given the *Slosson Intelligence Test,* which is of the Binet type although shorter. She earned an IQ of 91–93. Curiously, her main area of failure was that of number, over which she used elaborate avoidance techniques. Nor would she collaborate in the repetition of sentences. It was typical of her that although she could not, or would not tell the tester how many apples there were when there were only three, when the testing was over she drew 10 apples (see Fig. 3) and counted them correctly. She then drew the members of her family, with the correct number of children. Seeing the long ears she had given them she imaginatively called them pet rabbits. The drawings had good detail for a child just over 5 years, and there is no sign of any impairment in muscular control.

In September Jean entered kindergarten without fuss, and all went well for a few weeks. Thereafter she made another attempt at "control" by temper tantrums, and the teacher found her unmanageable. She was admitted to a childrens' psychiatric hospital some distance from her home, where she stayed for two months and attended school. After two months back at home she again proved unmanageable, and this time the mother was taken in with her for three weeks and given training in how to manage her. This followed the behavior-modification procedures that had been previously

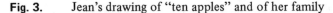

Fig. 3.   Jean's drawing of "ten apples" and of her family

including herself. Compare the hair-style of the

top left figure with her own in the photograph. (Fig. 1)

successful. During this period, the mother learned the behavior-modification principle of rewarding the child only when she behaved well. The next September, Jean entered Grade 1. There had never been any doubts about her mental ability.

Up to this point Jean's temperamental abnormality and consequent retardation have been discussed in terms of her volitions, that is to say, her chosen way of controlling her world. For the planning of a therapeutic program the chief desiderata are the patient's life-style and, when it is a question of combatting retardation, the learning style. In thus emphasizing the understanding and modification of behavior there is nevertheless a danger of falling into a purely behavioristic position, where everything is viewed in terms of conditioning from a *tabula rasa.* In fact, individual differences of temperament and hence of motivation cannot be wholly explained along such lines, and serious errors in treatment may arise if such assumptions are made. Notably, the extent of any constitutional impairment has also to be assessed, although this may become apparent only in the course of treatment. The style of behavior which the child is using at any one time is not necessarily the only one available. It may have been chosen in very early childhood owing to impairment or uneven development of the central nervous system; but over the ensuing years the damage or retardation may have been made good by the development of alternative structures, maturation, or biochemical stabilization. In such cases the potentiality for a more effective behavioral style may be present but lies dormant because the earlier style has established itself as the dominant one. This is particularly noticeable among impulsive, hyperactive children of kindergarten age whose problem-solving strategies are those of guessing or—in the event of difficulty—avoidance by distractibility. By means of a program which "punishes" such tactics and reinforces cognition it is often possible to bring the hitherto dormant good strategies into operation. In sum, the clinician has always to be assessing the potential repertoire of the child at a given stage of development.

Almost certainly, any grossly abnormal style of behavior in a child reared within a stable home environment can be traced to some initial impairment which has limited normal development. The diagnostic problem is that the subtle derangements of those parts of the nervous system which govern behavior are not anatomically observable. All we can do is note other indications of similarly subtle derangement in cognate structures, such as the motoric, speech and endocrine, and the reflexes controlling physical homeostasis. By the law of Multiple Congenital Impairment (Stott, 1966) such derangements confer a greater than chance probability of disturbance of the behavioral system.

Comprehensive diagnosis therefore requires as full an account as can be obtained of the child's developmental history. History-taking has fallen into disrepute because, being unsystematic, written reports differ greatly between one interviewer and another, and one can never be sure whether the absence of mention of a condition means that it was not present or whether the interviewer did not seek the information. In view of the need for a standard recording schedule the writer composed the *Systematic Interview Guides* (Stott,

1965) covering the pregnancy and the child's life up to 5 years.

In Jean's case we had to inquire why she alone of the five siblings chose such an incapacitating life-style. It is true that the mother reinforced her dependency and acted on the conviction that she was retarded. But her other four children resisted the temptation to exploit her overprotection, at least to the point of complete dependence.

In effect, Jean's history was characteristic of many retarded children. Mothers' accounts of the pregnancy are often suspect owing to the suspicion that with their child's defect in mind they think back in order to discover some cause. Drillien and Wilkinson (1964) found a way around this methodological difficulty by asking the mother right at the beginning of the interview to what she attributed the child's condition. They found that in three-quarters of the cases the mothers could not suggest any cause. The same device was used in the *Systematic Interview Guides*. The *Guide* asks a number of very specific questions concerning stresses and illnesses found to be associated with impairment in the child (Stott, 1957). These elicited that the mother had had an unhappy pregnancy. During the second month her father had to have surgery for a ruptured appendix. In the seventh the family moved to accommodate the husband's change of job, into a house that was cold and run down. They moved again when she was 8½ months pregnant. With her anxiety-prone temperament these events made her feel low and discouraged. During the year before Jean was born she had a duodenal ulcer and during the whole of the pregnancy suffered from indigestion.

Jean had a breech birth although she had been turned a week previously. Two weeks before the birth an amniocentesis was done to determine whether blood transfusion would be required, the mother being Rh-negative. For 48 hours after the birth the infant was incubated owing to mucous congestion, and a slight jaundice was noted for the first five days. She lay passive without spontaneous flexion and extension of the limbs.

Her childhood was free of serious illnesses, but she had chronic, nasal colds and an allergy to cow's milk that caused eczema. At 2½ years she suffered a single short *grand mal* seizure (her mother having had a series of such at exactly the same age).

Her developmental milestones were retarded. She did not

crawl until 12 months, nor walk across the room unaided before 27 months. She began to put 2 or 3 words together at 24 months. At 4 years she was sometimes difficult to understand because, as the mother put it, "the words seem to come all together," but she could speak clearly if she took the time. She had been more inclined than her siblings to hurt herself by falling or bumping into things, although by 4 years this was becoming less frequent. Just before this age, a psychiatrist diagnosed her as a mild case of cerebral palsy, but as we knew her she was normally coordinated. This clumsiness and the jumbled speech suggested a sequencing derangement rather than impairment of motor function as such.

Perhaps the most telltale impairment for the understanding of her later dependency needs was that she did not smile at people or show evidence of affection until she was 18 months old. From then on she became very clinging and could not bear to have her mother or other member of her family out of her sight. From about 2 years she lost her unnatural placidity and lethargy, and developed her pattern of temper tantrums followed by sulking. This excessive need for dependency and social interaction is not uncommon in children who fail to display normal early attachment behavior. It is tempting to conclude that they are belatedly making their way through the infantile phase of extreme dependency. All one can say for certain is that there was some derangement of the social-attachment behavior appropriate to each age.

A review of Jean's history suggests that she had suffered multiple congenital impairments of a minor character, affecting the central nervous system and especially the structures governing social behavior. However, these impairments seemed to be of the nature of faults in maturation. Given these, it is understandable that with her excessive needs for attachment after the age of 1½ years she became conditioned by her mother's overprotectiveness to exploit dependency and a guise of retardation as a means of social control which pervertedly satisfied her more-than-average need for effectiveness. In this sense she could be said to have "chosen" retardation as a life-style, but in another sense it could be argued that it was determined for her by a combination of congenital impairment and facilitating environment.

References

Benton, A.L. (1962). "Some aspects of the concept of psychogenic mental deficiency," *Proceedings of the London Conference on the Scientific Study of Mental Deficiency,* Dagenham, England: May and Baker, 243–250.

Chess, S. (1967). "The role of temperament in the child's development," *Acta Paedopsychiatric, 34,* 91–103.

Chess, S. (1968). "Temperament and learning ability of school children," *American Journal of Public Health, 58,* 2231–2239.

Downing, J. (1970). "Children's concepts of language in learning to read," *Educational Research, 12,* 106–112.

Drillien, C.M., and Wilkinson, E.M. (1964). "Emotional stress and mongoloid birth," *Developmental Med. and Child Neurol., 6,* 140–143.

Garfield, S.L., and Wittson, E. (1960). "Some reactions to the revised manual on terminology and classification in mental retardation," *American Journal of Mental Deficiency, 64,* 951–953.

Halpern, A.S. (1970). "Some issues concerning the differential diagnosis of mental retardation and behavior disturbance," *American Journal of Mental Deficiency, 74,* 796–800.

Heber, R. (1959). "A manual on terminology and classification in mental retardation," *American Journal of Mental Deficiency,* Monog. Supp. *64.*

Hunt, J. McV. (1961). *Intelligence and Experience,* New York: Ronald.

Murphy, L.B. (1962). *The Widening World of Childhood,* Chicago: Basic Books.

Nissen, H.W. (1958). "Axes of behavioral comparison," in A. Roe and G.G. Simpson (Eds.), *Behavior and Evolution,* New Haven, Conn.: Yale University Press.

Sontag, L.W. (1962). "Fetal behavior as a predictor of behavior in childhood," presentation to Annual Meeting of the American Psychiatric Association.

Stott, D.H. (1957). "Physical and mental handicaps following a disturbed pregnancy," *Lancet, 1,* (May 18), 1006–1012.

Stott, D.H. (1961). "An empirical approach to motivation based on the behavior of a young child," *Journal of Child Psychology and Psychiatry, 2,* 97–117.

Stott, D.H. (1962). *The Programmed Reading Kit,* Edinburgh: Holmes-McDougall.

Stott, D.H. (1965). *The Systematic Interview Guides,* London: University of London Press.

Stott, D.H. (1966). *Studies of Troublesome Children,* London: Tavistock; New York: Humanities Press.

Stott, D.H., and Sharp, J.D. (1968). *Effectiveness-Motivation scale,* available from Centre for Educational Disabilities, University of Guelph, Ontario.

Stott, D.H., and Sykes, E.G. (1971). *The Bristol Social Adjustment Guides,* London: University of London Press; San Diego: Educational and Industrial Testing Service, (Stott-Marston revision, 1971).

Stott, D.H. (1971a). *The Flying Start Learning-to-Learn Kit,* available from Centre for Educational Disabilities, University of Guelph, Ontario.

Stott, D.H. (1971b). *Guide to the Child's Learning Behavior,* available from Centre for Educational Disabilities, University of Guelph, Ontario.

Stott, DH. (1971c). *Manual to the Bristol Social Adjustment Guides,* 4th ed., London: University of London Press; San Diego: Educational and Industrial Testing Service.

White, R.W. (1959). "Motivation reconsidered: The concept of competence," *Psychology Review, 66,* 297–333.

Related Reading

Pseudo retardation

Benton, A.L. (1956). "The concept of pseudofeeblemindedness," *Archives of Neurology and Psychiatry; 75,* 379–388.

Burke, H.F. (1958). "Research of pseudo-mental retardation," in E.M. Bower and J.H. Rothstein (Eds.), *Problems in Mental Retardation, Sacramento:* California Department of Education, 40–43.

Phillips, E.L. (1957). "Contributions to a learning theory account of childhood autism," *Journal of Psychology, 43,* 117–124.

Stott, D.H. (1966). *Studies of Troublesome Children,* London: Tavistock, New York: Humanities Press

CHAPTER 4

Ken: An Indian Migrant Child

EVELYN P. MASON

Editor's Introduction

Ken is a multiple-disadvantaged: lower socioeconomic status, immigrant and semi-migrant, a member of a sub-group in an ethnic minority, partly bilingual, of a broken and unstable family structure, with a parental history of school failure or disinterest with prior grade level retention. If disadvantage is equated with limitations in the means for achieving health, occupational success, community recognition, and political impact, then Ken is a massively disadvantaged child. His problem reminds us that poverty, deficient health services and limited education were long associated with rural conditions. In recent years attention has gone chiefly to the urban and ghetto poor, but significant rural deprivation continues.

Some authorities list the Indian and some the migrant as "most educationally deprived." The two share many problems. Among Northwest Indians there is high infant mortality, twice the average level of hospitalization, a life expectancy probably below 46 years, and a welfare rate six times the local average (Fantini and Weinstein, 1968). Ken's family shares no full membership even in the Indian group. As a mixed family related to the Thompson, but not the local Lummi Indians, their nomadic rootlessness is unrelieved either by tribal community or neighboring with fully migrant groups.

The Indian often is described as suspended between two worlds, the tribe and the mass society. In this case there are few effects from an extended family or tribe. Ken, like other Indian children, has been present while important things went on, but there is little evidence that he has been influenced by story telling, advice, history, myth, and family affection (Spindler, 1963). In these ambiguous circumstances Ken has a mildly depressed self-concept, but it is clear that he has not given up faith in his own future. He has, instead, a powerful capacity to cope with the present, a self-trust found often among both rural and urban poor (Haggstrom, 1963; Eisenberg, 1963–4). Ken is not a disturbed person but one who lives in an environment which depreciates his potential.

There are two important questions concerning school intervention. Can it be efficient at age 14? If so, what should be the characteristics of the program?

The nation-wide attempt to overcome underprivilege and environmental monotony resulted in Head Start with an emphasis on early childhood. The outcomes have been mixed. Some of the small studies record notable success, but large scale studies do not show major and durable advances in academic facility (Weikart, 1967; Evans, 1971). No single answer may be given because some are short-term and some full-year experiments; it is possible that indirect outcomes override the apparent impermanence of academic gains.

It has been widely believed that educational backwardness in the lower class is induced and sustained by the prevalence of nonverbal and restrictive languages. Serviceable at home and in rote learning, this communication is redundant and inappropriate for long-term memory or planning. Convergent or restricted language is sustained in an environment which offers predetermined solutions and few alternatives (Bernstein, 1960). Ken has had small opportunity to acquire the formal or elaborated language with varied syntax which seems essential for logical and conceptual tasks.

The argument for delay in school intervention is based on the belief that autonomous learning skills come with early adolescence (Rohwer, 1971). At that point the child has maximum possibility for transcending the limits of early models. This argument may be extended to discount deliberate and pressured education in early childhood. Children may be "burned" or discouraged by their failures to please a teacher, and beyond that, formal school may reduce plasticity in children who have not developed mediating behavior and elaborative language. In short, the experts are not in agreement that *earliness* is an absolute and they are in disagreement over an appropriate pedagogy.

Supplementary summer programs for migrant children began in the 1940's and were supported by seven states in 1961 (Haney, 1963). The scholastic gains have been significant, and Project Catch Up followed these optimistic leads.

There are many bandwagons in the contemporary effort to provide relevant education to undo segregation, reduce poverty, and prevent social disorder. There are advocates of toughminded "catch-up" and assimilate. The argument is for early intervention to overcome cognitive deficiencies and promote the verbal and thinking strategies that place the learner in the mainstream of modern society (Hunt, 1961; Bereiter and Engelmann, 1966). Equally earnest arguments are made for a self-directed development of divergent codes with the enhancement of ethnic or group identity. In this view, differences are not deficits (Reissman, 1964; Baratz and Baratz, 1970). This latter position is sometimes translated to mean that there should be much concrete experience, more visual than aural presentation, and exploitation of situations and problems that have meaning in the child's daily life and possible future.

For some authorities, motive is the basic issue: classical and abstract studies are foreign in a picker's shack, but a teacher's smile or peer approval can be felt again when the light is out. Many teachers, therefore, advocate schools with intense affectivity; planned success experiences, touch rewards, sensitivity methods, personal references, group planning, and attempts to involve mothers. Additionally it is widely believed that power and organization matter, that minority parents must exert real power on curricular strategies and that parents must be teamed with staff.

Ken shows some depression of self-concept. It is widely accepted that self-valuation, in large part, regulates performance and action. It is also believed that this self-concept is inferred or learned through accumulated experience with significant others in the home and school. It is remarkably simple to condemn the school for failure to develop a positive image but it is also remarkably difficult to undo childish history, erase early perceptions, or shield the child from day-to-day conditions which depress his sense of self-worth. Superficial praise, easy assignments, or the use of a few examples from the child's own culture are small antidote against the realities (LaBenne and Greene, 1969). Ken's talents, his ability to cope at home, and his eagerness to succeed are positive elements but they are not easily put in the service of academic achievement.

A thoughtful reading of this case will leave teachers with many questions. Ken is a striking example of the difficulties encountered when diversity of students and multivariate purposes come together in schools.

MEETING KEN

It was a cold, rainy, gray spring morning when I drove in rural northwest Washington toward Nugent's Corner. Ken Charles' junior high counselor had said that the family had

a barrier to communication in recruitment, but the Project's success in the past had proven helpful in reducing communication problems. It became more and more apparent that Ken really did want to go but was almost afraid to consider the possibility.

We were still talking when his parents drove up in a nondescript, old car and entered the cabin with deliberate failure to notice us. I asked Ken if it were all right with him if I talked with them. He agreed, then bolted from the car and rushed into the cabin, probably to check and make sure everything was all right. Our knock was answered by Mr. Charles, a middle-aged Indian with a gray crew cut, a warm smile and a friendly manner. We were ushered quickly through the kitchen, a dark room with a wood stove, metal sink, a single faucet and sparse table and chairs, into the small room which doubled as living room and parents' bedroom. The furnishings included a double bed, an armchair and a television set. There was a lean-to room at the back which I learned was the bedroom for the three Charles children. There was no bathroom.

Mrs. Charles was perched on the bed. A small woman with a withered face and almost no upper teeth, she was dressed like her husband—working shirt, pants, and jacket. She seemed apprehensive and had little to say, but appeared interested. Mr. Charles took charge. He acknowledged that Ken's mother was reluctant to have him go, but assured me that if Ken really wanted to they would try to help him. He asked Ken if he would still be able to have his teeth fixed, and he wondered how Ken could get to the college campus, as the family undoubtedly would be working by then. Soon everyone was in agreement, releases were signed, transportation arrangements made, and the family was assured that additional information and directions would be sent before the Project began.

On the way out, Ken asked what kind of clothes he would need. I thought I heard him say he only had one suit. I quickly tried to reassure him that a suit was not necessary since the summer program was quite informal. The only clothes necessary would be jeans and a shirt or two. I did indicate that he should bring a warm jacket because we would be going on some camping trips. Then for the first time I looked closely at Ken's appearance. He had noticeably decaying teeth, but his evenly chiseled features, close cropped, neatly combed black hair, and freshly pressed wash pants and light jacket presented the impression of a well-groomed, ruggedly handsome youth.

Driving home my pleasurable ruminations about having secured Ken's participation were interrupted by my son's caustic remarks. "Mom, you shouldn't have made such an issue over the warm jacket. Didn't you hear him say he was wearing the only clothes he had? He doesn't have a warm jacket!"

I hadn't heard the message in just those terms, but Doug was right. Ken was wearing the only school clothes he had. They were the same clothes that had served on the five-mile trip to school during the cold winter months.

Doug offered other observations. He was impressed with Ken's manner. He remarked that if some strange woman had driven up to him in a big car when he was that age he would have been scared to death. Yet Doug felt Ken talked easily during the entire encounter. I wondered if this could reflect the years of experience Ken had talking with representatives from the Bureau of Indian Affairs, social workers from the Department of Public Assistance, or other agencies whose job it was to help the indigent. Or, was it a kind of independence he'd had to develop because of his circumstances?

THE PROGRAM

Ken's acceptance made him the 34th junior high student recruited of the 50 who would ultimately participate in the 1971 summer Project Catch-Up. Project participants are selected from referrals from all the junior high schools in northwest Washington state, primarily on the basis of teacher or counselor judgment. The criteria for nomination are evidence of academic potential, performance below ability level, and evidence of socioeconomic deficit. During the first year of the program, 1966, a fourth criterion had been stipulated: no evidence of severe emotional disturbance. Experience that first year demonstrated, however, that almost all the students were coping with some debilitating problems, both personal and social, and since there was no way to sort out which were the most disturbing, the criterion was dropped as unrealistic.

Recognition that in northwest Washington few American

Indian adolescents complete high school and that this same situation is occurring among the growing Chicano population was the stimulus for the initiation of Project Catch-Up. The program was designed to minimize the cumulative effects of previous academic failure, prejudicial social attitudes, and the pervasive results of economic deprivation. To accomplish this, efforts were directed toward altering negative self-concepts and poor motivational patterns, increasing decision-making capacities and ability to plan for the future, and developing responsibility. The program was implemented through a six-weeks residence program in an attractive college dormitory setting, considerable experience with academic success regardless of previous level of achievement, planned recreational and cultural enrichment, and individual and group counseling (Mason, 1968). The 1966–67 summer programs were designed as demonstration projects and the success of the first two summers primarily was measured by a significant reduction in expected school dropout rate (Mason, 1969b). To extend further the effects of the demonstration program, Project Catch-Up was redesigned to continue over five summers with intensive follow-up evaluation over ten years (Mason and Locasso, 1971). Ken's nomination to participate in the 1971 summer program occurred during the sixth year of the Project.

SETTLING IN

On the first Sunday of the program, staff members are assigned participants whose families cannot bring them to the dormitory. As I had called on the Charles family during the recruitment procedures, I volunteered to pick up Ken. It was a warm, sunny day when I arrived. Both the Charles' and the Gonzales' families were milling about between the two cabins. The adults had obviously been drinking. Ken was impatiently waiting with his suitcase, carefully dressed and wearing a light blue, freshly laundered warm jacket.

Goodbyes were said hastily and Ken climbed into the car. The half-hour trip to the college was filled with Ken's staccato account of his background—almost as if his mother or someone had given him all his vital statistics just the night before so he would know who he was. At first I questioned the validity of some of his statements, but later I learned to accept Ken's matter-of-fact reports of startling events as part of his almost fatalistic resignation.

Ken immediately wanted me to notice the warm jacket. His family had pooled their resources and had been able to buy some second hand clothes in "Old Town." He would need transportation to the dentist in mid-July for his first extractions, but he was only going to have his upper teeth out and the July extractions would only be the back ones. His school had arranged for both his sister and Ken to have dentures through the Hamilton Fund. He was pleased because this would not only improve his appearance but he would be more comfortable. It hurt when food got into the cavities.

His mother was just out of the hospital. His uncle next door had knocked her down and kicked her in the stomach when his dad had neglected to fix his uncle's car like he had promised. His dad had been asleep in the next room when it happened but he hadn't done anything. It wasn't his real dad. He wasn't sure who his real dad was. His mother, his two sisters, and Ken had lived with his grandmother in Canada when he was young.

In response to my inquiry about where this was, he remembered that it was across the border a little way in a small Indian village close to Boston Bar, off the Thompson River Indian reservation. In fact his little sister, who is just younger than his little brother, was there now with his grandmother.

I indicated surprise that he had more than one sister and he mentioned for the first time that another sister just younger than he had died in the hospital last year. He thought it was a brain tumor but he wasn't sure. He really missed her.

Then he changed back to talking about Mr. Charles. He was like his dad. They had been together over three years now. If his mother died first Mr. Charles had promised to raise Ken like his own son. Only to become his *real* son Ken would have to learn Mr. Charles' language. Ken wasn't sure if this would be possible for him because he didn't know Indian languages and Mr. Charles never used his. His grandmother did, however, so maybe he could learn it.

As we neared the campus, Ken turned his attention to the coming summer program. He understood that there was some question about whether he would be able to go into the eighth grade unless he did well this summer so he was really going to work hard. He had already "failed" one grade and he didn't want to be held back again. School was important to him.

He wanted the reassurance that all the kids and the staff would be living in the dormitory. He was curious about whether he would know any of the other kids and if he would have a roommate. He also wanted to know about activities other than school classes. Walking down the steps toward the Ridgeway dormitory complex, Ken became noticeably quieter. Finally he blurted out, "Is this it? Is this the dormitory? I didn't know it would be so big. Why, it's just like a big motel!"

Ken was greeted by one of the junior counselors who took him to his room. They picked up bedding and towels on the way and the counselor showed Ken how to make his bed, where to hang his clothes and reminded Ken that most of the rooms were alike with two single beds, two desks, and two closets. Ken volunteered nervously that he's never before slept in a bed by himself.

The rest of the initial day was set aside to acquaint the participants with the dormitory, the campus, other students and staff. As families and youngsters were arriving and leaving, I noticed Ken nervously walking from room to room. On one occasion he did confide that he had found one other Indian boy he knew. Even so, he seemed to have little to do with other participants, he appeared tense, and despite the temperature, he did not remove the warm jacket. The Co-Director of the Project sensed Ken's concern and invited him into his apartment to get acquainted. Ken spent the first night on the couch in the Co-Director's living room.

The next day the students were introduced to classes in language arts, computational skills, science, and elective projects such as industrial arts, crafts, photographjy, and sewing. Possible recreational activities were outlined in the afternoon and in a general meeting of participants and staff the expectations of participants, of staff and of the program were discussed. The large group then was divided into smaller groups which later became the base for bi-weekly group counseling sessions. These small group meetings were concluded with a discussion of tasks to be accomplished the following day, a day of objective tests.

PROGRAM EXPECTATIONS

In the controversial area of educational programs for the disadvantaged, one persistent issue raised has been the question of whether innovative educational experiences do, in fact, effect changes in behavior. Those individuals concerned with early learning maintain that if change is to occur at all, environmental manipulation must be introduced at an early age (Hebb, 1949; Deutsch, 1963; Bloom, 1964; Piaget, 1964). Others, while recognizing that early intervention has the argument of efficiency, insist that changes in cognitive development, academic achievement, personality characteristics, vocational interests, and ability to plan for the future can be effected if sufficient opportunity for new learning is presented to the adolescent (Hunt, 1961; Ausubel, 1964; Wolin, 1969). And still another point of view is that little change, if any at all, can be effected by new intensified educational experiences (Jensen, 1969).

Even though the participants in the first two summers of Project Catch-Up showed significant gains over the summer months in academic skills (measured by standardized tests) these gains were lost when the students returned to their usual school situations (measured by mean grade point averages) (Mason, 1969b). Beginning in 1968, measures of intellectual functioning, academic achievement, and personality characteristics were administered at the beginning of each summer program and subsequently in the spring of the following year. The test measures used were the *California Test of Mental Maturity* (Sullivan, Clark and Tieggs, 1947), *California Achievement Tests of Reading and Arithmetic* (Tieggs and Clark, 1957), and the *California Psychological Inventory* (Gough, 1957).

The usefulness of standardized tests with disadvantaged students had been severely criticized by educators and psychologists. Different vocabularies, limited reading abilities, and particularly bi-lingual home backgrounds are known to produce test scores that are inadequate measures of actual ability levels. On the other hand, since the young people participating in Project Catch-Up are enrolled during the academic year in usual public school classrooms their scores on standardized tests do give some indication of their relative position in comparison to other classmates (Fishman, Deutsch, Kogan, North, and Whitehead, 1964). The use of standardized tests, then, was justified on the basis of giving some measure of comparative functioning when they came to the program. Also, these tests allowed objective measurement of change in performance, if any occurred, over the academic year after the project.

Statistical analyses of the pre- and post-testings for the 1968 and 1969 participant groups did, in fact, show improved academic achievement, continued development in mental maturity, and evidence of improved evaluations of self-worth over time. Admittedly the mean post-test scores for both groups was below grade placement, but the statistically significant increment in performance was of importance in light of the consistent evidence that academic achievement for the disadvantaged adolescents either remains stationary or declines. Evidence of slightly greater improvement among the 1968 and 1969 girl participants and of superior performance for Anglos, with Indians consistently lower were additional important findings (Mason and Locasso, 1971).

KEN'S PARTICIPATION

The intent on the day of testing was explained as clearly as possible to the 1971 participants and they were encouraged to marshal their resources so that they might perform to the best of their ability. They were to be divided into small groups so that the tests could be administered with as much individual attention as the standardized instructions would allow. Also, because of the length and the vocabulary level of the *California Psychological Inventory,* the questions were to be read orally and the students asked to mark their true or false responses on answer sheets.

Next morning the 1971 "Catch-Uppers" as they were now calling themselves entered the testing situation with a happy, cooperative attitude. However, despite breaks for cold drinks, lunch, and a couple of walks around the building, it proved to be a long day. Ken worked diligently and seemed unusually careful in his attempts to make sure he understood all the directions. He obviously wanted to do well, but simultaneously seemed somewhat baffled by what was expected of him. After the testing and before dinner, Ken stopped to visit with the Co-Director and other staff members in the apartment. Ken seemed more comfortable with staff than he was with the other participants. Even his roommate, an Anglo boy, seemed to pose a threat.

The following day was to set the pace for the rest of the summer program. The daily morning schedule was divided so that all participants rotated through the three classes of science, language arts, and math. Science was held in one of the college biology laboratories, but was organized so that the instructor and her assistants could help the students initiate and develop individual projects based on their own interests. Language arts instruction was almost on an individual basis with fellows in a Reading Consultant Program as instructors. The three math instructors held their class in the living room of the dormitory. Games using number skills were used, and students were encouraged to contract for the amount of work they planned to accomplish each class period, asking for assistance from the instructors only when needed. Instruction in all areas began at the proficiency level of the student and moved ahead as rapidly as the student seemed able to go.

Attendance at class was voluntary. The expectation that the students would assume responsibility for class attendance was made clear, however. As always, getting the young people up in the morning proved difficult. Many were not in the habit of eating breakfast and some of the Indian young people awoke fully dressed. They had learned early in life that because of potential fire hazard in their homes, it was safer to go to bed fully clothed. In contrast to the grumblings and bad tempers of some of the young people, however, Ken was quick to get up, make his bed, and dress carefully. In fact, he frequently changed his clothes during the day and was always a little ahead of schedule in keeping his clothes laundered. Showers seemed a particular joy to him.

Ken's attendance at class was punctual and he was always willing to attempt new tasks. These conscientious efforts were frequently frustrated, however, because obviously he was unskilled in fundamentals of reading and math. Almost immediately evident as an additional limitation was his attempt to memorize situations and answers with little attention to the context or the process for solution of the problem. Somewhere along the line, Ken had identified having the right answer, regardless of source, as the main criterion for success.

Substantiation for these observations was available with the return of the test results. On the *California Test of Mental Maturity* Ken achieved a nonlanguage I.Q. of 99, a language I.Q. of 81, and a total I.Q. of 91, showing measured intellectual functioning within the average to low average range. His performance, however, in comparison to other Indian participants was above average. It was assumed, then, recognizing the limitations of the test instrument, that Ken's intellectual potential was considerably above that of the test measures.

As expected, academic achievement levels were critically low in some areas. On the *California Reading Test* Ken's scores ranged from the 4.4 grade level (general reading vocabulary) to the 7.0 grade level (following instructions) with an overal placement at the 5.5 grade level. While somewhat more proficient in arithmetic (performance ranging from 5.0 grade level for division to 8.4 grade level for meanings) his overall arithmetic achievement was at the 6.5 grade level. Hoping to gain insight into how Ken felt about himself, not only in relation to his academic achievement but also personally, we attended to his scores on the *California Psychological Inventory* (see Fig. 1).

With the intent to understand better some of the problems the participants in Project Catch-Up are facing, we regularly study personality characteristics of the ethnic groups as one aspect of the research evaluation. Since the *California Psychological Inventory* (CPI) provides measures of a selected number of "folk concepts" judged to be important determiners of positive, socially constructive behavior, it was decided to use this instrument to measure attitudes toward self, level of social maturity, and achievement motivation. Scores from true-false responses to the 480 statements of the CPI yield 18 scales. These are dominance, capacity for status, sociability, social presence, self-acceptance, sense of well-being, responsibility, socialization, self-control, tolerance, good impression, communality, achievement via conformity, achievement via independence, intellectual efficiency, psychological mindedness, flexibility, and femininity.

Statistical analysis of the CPI test scores obtained during the first two summer programs showed a significant overall ethnic difference ordered with the Anglos highest and the Indians lowest. The pattern of the variability of attitudes expressed by the Mexicans suggested that even though these young people voice some positive feelings about their ability to achieve in the areas of social conformity, their predominant view of self-worth was almost as negative as the Indian view (Mason, 1969a).

A surprising consistency in the statistical analyses of the CPI test scores was evidenced in the analyses of the 1968, 1969, and 1970 participant groups. In addition to the cross-validated overall *ethnic* difference, a generalized more negative response by *females* regardless of ethnic background was evidenced. Possibly because females mature at an earlier age, their acceptance of an essentially hopeless outlook is more fixed. Of further interest was the consistent interaction of ethnic group and the subscale "tolerance".

Fig. 1

RESPONSES OF A 14 YEAR OLD INDIAN BOY TO THE CALIFORNIA PSYCHOLOGICAL INVENTORY AT THE BEGINNING OF THE 1971 PROJECT CATCH-UP COMPARED TO THE AVERAGE RESPONSE OF THE AMERICAN INDIAN ADOLESCENT FROM PRECEDING PROJECTS

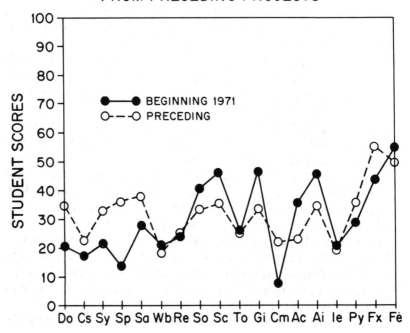

The relationship between negative overall response to the CPI and low scores on tolerance suggested that those individuals who experience the greatest prejudice from others respond with a corresponding degree of intolerance (Mason and Locasso, 1971).

But the greatest importance in all of the samples was the consistent evidence of complete passivity, negative feelings of self-worth, and social ineptness reported by both male and female Indians. It would appear that the prejudicial attitudes the Indian encounters rob him of personal initiative and self-respect.

INCREASED INVOLVEMENT

Ken's CPI profile (see Fig. 1) showed scores on scales measuring feelings of social competency (dominance, capacity for status, sociability, social presence, self-acceptance, and feeling of well-being) as *below* the average Indian response. Noteworthy, however, was his response to the scale measuring feelings of well-being, which was no lower than the Indian average. Further, on the scales measuring social responsibility (responsibility, socialization, and self-control) Ken responded more positively. He was more concerned about creating a good impression than the average, but felt less able to conform to peer standards (communality). His attitudes toward achieving were about average, but his feelings about his intellectual efficiency were similar to the average Indian adolescent. At the beginning of the program, then, by comparison to the average, negative Indian response to the CPI, Ken saw himself as even more passive and less confident socially, but he felt more responsible and showed more motivation to achieve.

Just as the tests of intellectual functioning and school achievement helped to describe some of the problems Ken was encountering even in the more relaxed classroom situations of Project Catch-Up, the CPI profile was descriptive of some of his behavioral responses to the summer program. From the beginning Ken was a delight to the staff. He was careful to follow instructions, was responsible and pleasant. He conversed freely with participants and staff; yet, he was soon recognized as a "loner." Ken's relationship with his roommate was one of friendly indifference, and when the time came to change roommates Ken moved into a single room.

Ken continued to make efforts to involve himself in the program. Even though initially hesitant to participate in recreational activities, with guidance and assurance that he could swim or sail or manage on a camping trip, soon he was volunteering and signing up for new activities. Staff rating of his sociability went from very low to high during the summer, but close friendships and confidential conversations remained primarily with adults.

On the second week-end of the program, parents were invited to visit the dormitory to talk with staff and see their children. Ken's parents arrived in mid-afternoon and stayed until dinner. In the late afternoon Ken voiced a concern about papers he had left at home which he would need before his dental appointment the following week. A junior counselor offered to drive Ken home to pick up the papers. She reported later that she had been unaware of Ken's parents' visit and when she and Ken arrived at his home Ken explained his parents' absence by assuming that they were still hitch-hiking back from the dormitory. She voiced surprise and annoyance that Ken had not mentioned his parents' need for transportation. Ken said he did not want to bother the other staff.

Ken's academic progress continued to be slow. Despite his efforts, which sometimes seemed to be self-defeating, he could not seem to unlock himself from the anticipation of failure. He confided to one staff member that his early school attendance had been irregular and he often felt out of place in school. For the last three years his school attendance had been better, however, and he did feel his present school counselor was understanding.

Wilford Wasson, Director of Indian Studies, College of Ethnic Studies, Western Washington State College, has some telling observations on hindrances to Indian education (1970). He lists the following characteristics as common to many Indian students:

1. English in many cases is a second language. An Indian child who learned an Indian language first and English later will have trouble with communication, but even the Indian who has never spoken anything but English will have problems. He learned English from Indian parents, and his grammar may be different and certain words may have different connotations. There are many subtleties of

white middle class communication with which he is not familiar, and there is just as much nonverbal communications among Indians which is lost on the white teacher.

2. Indian students generally have a low self-concept. Everything an Indian child comes in contact with, outside his own community, tells him he is inferior. When everyone with whom you associate treats you as inferior, you soon begin to think of yourself as inferior. Average family income of $1500 per year, average life expectancy of 44 years, an unemployment rate ten times the national average all contribute to the low self-concept.

3. Indian students are not accustomed to high competition, particularly as it occurs in the classroom. Indians are primarily a cooperative rather than a competitive group . . . Many teachers unknowingly use competition to motivate, but rather than motivate the Indian student, competition simply turns him off. Different value systems are perceived. White teachers in the past have operated on the assumption that their values and morals are universal truths . . . Teachers, in the name of orderliness, are forcing Indian students to conform to value systems that are not their own and that sometimes are abhorrent to them.

4. Indian students may lack social supports for academic achievement . . . An Indian child first approaches school with enthusiasm and anticipation, but finds that the school has little to offer him. Since the parents have had similar experiences, there is little encouragement from home. His peer group is in the same situation so it gives no encouragement. Many teachers do not expect academic excellence from the Indian student . . . The author's third grade teacher told him that he could not expect to keep up with the white students, but if he would sit in the back of the room and not create a disturbance, he would be passed . . .

5. Indian students lack successful academic role models. Very few Indians in the past have graduated from college, and most of those have had to leave the reservation to find employment. Only one percent of the teachers of Indian children are Indian. There are practically no Indian college professors. Without these visible role models, there is no evidence for the Indian child that academic success is possible. He never sees his people in positions of authority, only in subservient roles.

Even though many of the problems facing the American Indian are common to all, subtle variations in tribal cultures may influence successful educational innovations (Zintz,

1962). For the most part the Indian participants in Project Catch-Up have represented the Lummi, Nooksack, Swinomish, Tulalip, and other coastal Indian tribes. The Thompson River Indian tribe, in contrast, is classified as part of the plateau Indian culture. Admittedly, any attempt to generalize tribal customs over a large geographic area results in over-simplification. Nevertheless, a dominant trend in the tribal units of the plateau Indians has been a concern with pacifism and the equality of men (Owens, Deets and Fisher, 1967). Tribal customs dictated that from earliest infancy children be drilled in the tenets of peaceful existence. The pugnacious man was ostracized.

Groups of 10 or 20 persons lived together over periods of many years without serious altercation, with the safety valve provided that a person could leave at any time and find a home elsewhere. Insignificant matters and major problems alike were decided with reference to what action would make for the greatest harmony. For example, the man who decided not to take revenge upon his brother who had stolen his wife, was commended for his decision.

COMPLETION AND EVALUATION

The dental extraction of Ken's back teeth was successfully accomplished during the middle part of the program. He was out of action for a time and spent his nights on the couch in the Co-Director's apartment but he did not complain. During the summer he was bothered occasionally by tension headaches but this problem lessened as the summer progressed.

On the fourth Sunday of the project, parents again were invited to visit. This time Mrs. Charles arrived with Eileen, Ken's sister, and a friend of the family. Ken was pleased to see them and readily escorted them around the campus. He encouraged Eileen to talk with one of the staff members about a program for high school students and introduced them all to other participants. Ken seemed slightly more comfortable with the girls in the program but was obviously beginning to enjoy the companionship of his peers.

Ken's academic instructors were pleased with his progress by the end of the program. He had made measurable gains but was still frustrated by limited basic skills. Even with these frustrations, however, he appeared to be feeling more positively about the possibility of success.

At the end of the program, Ken himself was enthusiastic. He had had a good summer. He, like the other young people, wanted to stay longer but, unlike many of the others, he did not voice an unwillingness to go home. Some of these feelings were more graphically illustrated in Ken's responses to a second CPI administered during the last class day of the program.

Figure 2 shows that Ken was significantly more positive in response to the second test than he was to the first CPI, his attitudes about his competencies in the areas of dominance, capacity for status, sociability, social presence, self-acceptance, communality and psychological mindedness, all of which clearly indicated that Ken felt more positively about his ability to function as a social being. He was slightly less positive in his views as they related to socialization, self-

Fig. 2

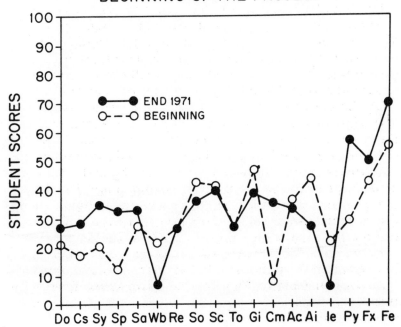

RESPONSES OF A 14 YEAR OLD INDIAN BOY TO THE CALIFORNIA PSYCHOLOGICAL INVENTORY AT THE END OF THE 1971 PROJECT CATCH–UP COMPARED TO HIS RESPONSES MADE AT THE BEGINNING OF THE PROJECT

control, and good impression, but rather than indicating a lessening in feelings of responsibility, these differences suggested greater flexibility in his functioning, a hypothesis supported by his slightly higher response to the flexibility scale. Despite these marked social gains, Ken was noticeably more negative in his responses to scales of feelings of well-being, achievement, and intellectual efficiency. It seemed that his greater awareness of his performance proficiency was reality oriented but depressing, and of concern to him personally.

On the last day of the Project, parents with transportation picked up their children while the staff arranged rides for others. Just as Ken was leaving with one of the counselors, Mr. and Mrs. Charles, Eileen, and the Gonzaleses appeared. Their surprise appearance reminded the staff that despite difficulties, the Charles family, particularly Mrs. Charles, had always made the effort to visit or to support Ken. Ken's parents were obviously pleased with the positive reports of Ken's successes, but voiced a concern that it would be quite a contrast for Ken to return to working in the fields. Ken assured them that he needed the money for school and they all went away seemingly quite happy.

After the participants leave, the staff spends the following week compiling reports to be sent to the referring schools. Some communication is maintained with the young people by letter or telephone, but actual follow-ups and follow-through efforts are not initiated until school begins.

During the report writing week some staff comments about Ken were:

"Hungry for approval."

"If you couldn't do what he asked you to do he'd get up and do it for himself."

"Very sensitive and easily hurt."

"Seemed to be taken advantage of by some of the kids because of his own mildness."

"Related well with adults—has trouble relating to peers."

"Interested first in interacting with girls—later with the boys." The summary of these reports sent to the schools was:

Affective: One staffer put it—"tremendous social gains." Very independent on arrival but displayed a lack of social interaction capacities. A loner. At the end of the six weeks totally involved in all aspects of the program. For us, a real success story.

Cognitive: Good attendance. Tried everything—in many instances failed because of the lack of background skills. Willing but needs real support and assistance for a time. *Rating on Semantic Differential:* overall growth, high; academic participation, high; social interaction, high; social and intellectual independence, high.

BACK TO SCHOOL

In the interim between the end of Project Catch-Up and the beginning of school only a brief contact was made with Ken. He had had the remainder of his teeth out and was not feeling well. Thus the frantic call from Ken's school counselor when school began was not expected. She was uncertain about her information, but was afraid Ken was living alone. Mrs. Gonzales was in the next cabin but was due to go to the hospital at any time to deliver her third baby. Ken, as the only other "adult" there, was to stay home from school to take care of the Gonzales' children.

The field representative for Project Catch-Up went out to see Ken that evening. Ken's matter-of-fact report of happenings revealed that his mother had left with the "friend of the family," Eileen had left with Mr. Gonzales, his father was east of the mountains working in the apples, and his grandmother had taken his little brother to Canada. He had no money and very little food, but he couldn't leave because his parents would not know where he was when they returned. Besides, his aunt needed him.

During the next week, Ken's school attendance was regular though it must have been difficult for him as his denture was not to be ready for another three weeks. His counselor was concerned about Ken's assuming complete responsibility for the younger Gonzales children during his aunt's stay in the hospital, but was beginning to realize that he was quite capable of so doing. Ken did call the Project office once during that week. He wanted to know if the field representative could leave some of the candle-making materials he'd used during the summer at his school. He didn't have money to buy his aunt a birthday present.

Following usual procedures, the school notified the Department of Public Assistance to inquire whether a foster home for Ken was a legal necessity. The social worker assigned to the case could not go out that week but would manage an appointment the next week. By this time the school counselor had learned from Eileen that she was in Canada and planned to return the following week-end. The counselor was obviously concerned about Eileen's future education as well, but, in addition, she was aware that it would be easier for Ken to have his sister at home.

Eileen did return and Mrs. Gonzales did have her baby. The conversation with the Department of Public Assistance social worker after her visit to the Charles' home was punctuated with "oh mys," "oh dears," and "This is so complicated," but nevertheless the general consensus was that despite their minor status, the Charles children were managing quite well on their own.

Since this time Mr. Charles has returned. Mr. Gonzales is home, and though Mrs. Charles and her friend are in a nearby town, it is thought that they too will return.

The plight of the whole Charles family is not much different from that of many Indian families. Caught between tribal teachings of their ancestors and the expectations of the white man's culture, Mr. and Mrs. Charles are reluctant to return to their reservation where there are no jobs but simultaneously they have neither the skills nor the education to secure employment that will provide an adequate income. Alcohol becomes a frequent sedative.

Ken, his sister Eileen, and the younger Charleses have functioned most of their lives in this double bind. In some ways these young people have become more knowledgeable than their parents, are more independent and responsible, and have learned to care for themselves. But these accomplishments have taken their toll in feelings of inferiority, hypersensitivity, difficulty in relating to peers, and now Ken's nervous headaches which bothered him slightly during the summer are occurring more frequently. Will Ken survive his circumstances? Will he achieve his present goal of becoming a language arts instructor? He has a lot going for him. Ken has a real sense of family identity as he defines it. Obviously his grandmother has been the focal point of family stability, but Ken also feels the loyalty and support of his mother and aunt. He is in a good school situation with teachers and a counselor who understand. And he has the support of Project Catch-Up.

But the family may have to move. The public health officer

is insisting that the berry farmer put in hot water and bath-rooms. Mr. Charles has no other winter employment. If a move is necessary, their only choice will be to return to the Indian village close to Boston Bar, off the Thompson River Indian reservation, where they can live on Public Assistance checks.

References

Ausubel, D.P. (1964)."How reversible are the cognitive and motivational effects of cultural deprivation? Implications for teaching the cultur-ally deprived child," *Urban Education, 1,* 16–38.

Baratz, S., and Baratz, J. (1970) "Early childhood intervention: the social science of institutional racism," *Harvard Educational Review, 40,* 29–50.

Bereiter, C., and Engelmann, S. (1966). *Teaching the Disadvantaged Child in the Pre-school,* Englewood Cliffs, N.J.: Prentice Hall.

Bernstein, B. (1960). "Language and social class," *British Journal of Sociology, 11,* 271–276.

Bloom, B.S. (1964). *Stability and Change in Human Characteristics,* New York: Wiley.

Deutsch, M. (1963). "The disadvantaged child and the learning process," in A.H. Passow (Ed.), *Education in Depressed Areas,* New York: Teachers College, Columbia University, 163–180.

Eisenberg, L. (1963–4). "Strengths of the inner city child," *Baltimore Bulletin of Education, 41,* 10–16.

Evans, E. (1971). *Contemporary Influences in Early Childhood Education,* New York: Holt, Rinehart and Winston.

Fantani, M.D., and Weinstein, G. (1968). *The Disadvantaged: Challenge to Education,* New York: Harper and Row, 65–66.

Fishman, J., Deutsch, M., Kogan, L., North, R., and Whitehead, M. (1964). "Guidelines for testing minority group children," *Journal of Social Issues, 20,* 129–145.

Gough, H.G. (1957). Manual for the *California Psychological Inventory,* Palo Alto: Consulting Psychologist Press.

Haggstrom, W.C. (1963). "The power of the poor," in A.H. Passow (Ed.), *Education in Depressed Areas,* New York: Bureau of Publications, Teachers College, Columbia University, 205–222.

Haney, G.E. (1963) "Problems and trends in migrant education," *School Life, 45,* 5–9.

Hebb, D.O. (1949). *The Organization of Behavior,* New York: Wiley.

Hunt, J.McV. (1961). *Intelligence and Experience,* New York: Ronald Press, 362–363.

Jensen, A.R. (1969). "How much can we boost I. Q. and scholastic achieve-ment?," *Harvard Education Review, 39,* 1–123.

LaBenne, W.D., and Greene, B.I. (1969). *Educational Implication of Self-Concept Theory,* Pacific Palisades, Calif.: Goodyear.

Mason, E.P. (1968). "Progress report: Project Catch-Up," *Psychology in the Schools, 5,* 272–276.

Mason, E.P. (1969a). "Cross-validation study of personality characteristics of junior high students from American Indian, Mexican, and Caucasian ethnic backgrounds," *Journal of School Psychology, 77,* 15–24.

Mason, E.P. (1969a). "Project Catch-Up: An educational program for socially disadvantaged thirteen and fourteen year olds," *Psychology in the Schools, 6,* 253–257.

Mason, E.P., and Locasso, R.M. (1971). "Evaluation of potential for change in junior high age youth from American Indian, Mexican, and Anglo ethnic backgrounds," report, Western Washington State College, Bellingham, Wash.

Owen, R., Deets, J., and Fisher, A. (1967) *The North American Indians,* New York: Macmillan, 170–178.

Piaget, J. (1964). "Development and learning," in R.D. Ripple and V.A. Rockcastle, (Eds.), *Piaget Rediscovered,* Ithaca, N.Y.: Cornell University.

Reissman, F. (1964). "The strategy of style," *Teachers College Record, 65,* 484–489.

Rohwer, W.D., Jr. (1971). "Prime time for education: early childhood or adolescence," *Harvard Educational Review, 41,* 316–341.

Spindler, G.D. (1963). "Personality, sociocultural system and education among the Menomi," in G.D. Spindler, (Ed.), *Education and Culture, Anthropological Approaches,* New York: Holt, Rinehart and Winston, 351–399.

Sullivan, E.T., Clark, W.W., and Tieggs, E.W. (1947). *Manual for California Test of Mental Maturity,* Monterey, Calif.: California Test Bureau.

Tieggs, E.W., and Clark, W.W. (1957). *Manual for California Achievement Test,* Monterey, Calif.: California Test Bureau.

Wasson, W. (1970). "Hindrances of Indian Education," *Educational Leadership: 28,* 278–280.

Weikart, D. (1967). *Preschool Intervention: A Preliminary Report of the Perry Preschool Project,* Ann Arbor, Mich.: Campus Publisher.

Wolin, M. (1969). "Group care: friend or foe?," *Social Work, 4,* 35–52.

Zintz, M.V. (1962). "Problems of classroom adjustment of Indian children in public schools in the Southwest," *Science Education, 46, 216–269.*

Related Readings

Barry, B. (1968). *The Education of American Indians,* Washington D.C.: U.S. Department of Health, Education and Welfare.

Bloom, B.S., Davis, A., and Hess, R.D. (1965). *Compensatory Education for Cultural Deprivation,* New York: Holt, Rinehart and Winston.

Deloria, V., Jr. (1969). *Custer Died for Your Sins,* New York: Macmillan.

Passow, A.H., Goldberg, M. and Tannenbaum, A.J. (Eds.) (1967). *Education of the Disadvantaged,* New York: Holt, Rinehart and Winston.

Selinger, D. (1968). *The American Indian Graduate; After High School What?,* Portland, Ore.: Northwest Regional Educational Laboratory.

Steiner, S. (1967). *The New Indians,* New York: Harper & Row.

U.S. Congress, Senate Special Subcommittee on Indian Education, *Indian Education: A National Tragedy, A National Challenge,* Washington D.C.: U.S. 91st Congress, 1st Session, Report 1969, 91–501.

CHAPTER 5

Kristen: A Dreadful Problem

DIANA DAVIS
MADELINE REID

Editor's Introduction

The Kristen story is like classic tragedy in which the central figure is swept by unmanageable forces toward inevitable failure. The authors do not identify their own theoretical position but the case can be readily related to the dynamic or Freudian model. Many modern psychologists dismiss these notions as nonsense or at most, allow that Freud made some shrewd observations on development and personal crises. Nevertheless, it is with victims and with deeply disturbed patients that psychoanalytic ideas seem most valid.

The dynamic model has been used to interpret widely separated functions, to explain creativity, and to guide therapy with repressed patients (Shakow and Rapaport, 1954; Kneller, 1965). Both creative and pathological acts have been explained as barbaric bursts, the outcome of energies driven underground by social constraints and then erupting in new and unrecognized forms. If libidinal and aggressive drives find no acceptable outlet, the content becomes unconscious and henceforth is poorly understood, little modified by reasoning, and remarkably persistent. The balance of energies and the distribution of attention move away from the norm and they reduce the conscious system to a mask for unconscious purposes.

Analysts have maintained that sex and aggression differ from other drives because their satisfaction excites social concern and involves others but also because these drives are most susceptible to distortion. Analytic case material includes cases of seductive or sadistic parents acting out their own neurotic needs through children. This is perceived as a major source of primitive antisocial reactions in the children (Johnson and Szurek, 1952). Nevertheless, problems such as Kristen's may spring less from malicious or unconscious abuse than from generally defective parenting. Before a child has learned differentiations, especially differentiation between *"self"* and *"other"* analysts explain that the child is flooded with emotions from the other. In this period children incorporate feelings and characteristics of people who care for them. Kristen may be one who responded to very early tensions between the parents or may be a special child not cared for or comforted enough. If she was thwarted in the first out-turnings of affection, her behavior now may include regressions to archaic anger. A 1946 study in Illinois found three patterns in recorded information for patients in a child guidance clinic (Hewitt and Jenkins, 1946). One cluster seems descriptive of Kristen's case, a constellation of solitariness, unsocialized aggression, and parental rejection.

Karl Menninger has described special personality deformations as "frozen emergency reactions" (Menninger, Wayman and Pruyser, 1963). The threatened person adopts an emergency measure as a permanent way of life. These responses are naturally extreme and they maintain both defective thinking and faulty human relations. Other specialists have described development of a shallow or pathologic mood short in nuances and lacking normal restrictions unsuited to learning, and not subject to reality testing (Jacobson, 1957). The suggested cause of these moods is an intense experience with resulting energy overflow and spread of feelings to all objects and relations. The mood becomes a groundwork for inappropriate strong responses.

Some readers will find special meaning in Kristen's fascination with death or the possible symbolism of a gun shooting through slits of the window. Kristen feared being alone with the doors shut. It is possible that she feared herself so that the enclosure was a microcosm of a threatening life situation. Samples of her writing (included) expose loneliness and sense of failure at self-management.

The closing incidents are so abnormal and so related to other elements in the case, that the reader is tempted to say "Aha, the key!" but caution is in order. The parental relation with the child surely is important but it may not be fundamentally generic. It could be just another piece in a complex of defects. There were problems before this generation, and Kristen's difficulties are reported to initiate in the first few months probably before she was able to differentiate *self* from *mother*. They at least antedate what is thought to be the major period of paternal influence. The whole fabric of life was distorted. The marriage itself may have been held together by reciprocal abnormalities. Each fragment helps to suggest an etiology, but gives little directive for therapy.

This child has been the object of concern on every side, she has consumed the energies of school, mental health, enforcement, and well-intentioned people but all for "no gain." Kristen is left with a very limited strategy for life. She is equipped with only the primitive modes of self-defense and we are unsure what ghosts or enemies threaten her.

INTRODUCTION

Tall and narrow, almost wiry in build, skin tinted by freckles which in certain lights almost disappeared, Kristen gave the impression that her personal appearance was of little account to her; her care of herself was functional rather than decorative. She had chronically bitten fingernails, a large boil-like eruption on her leg, small flat facial features, and brown hair tipped with the remnants of apricot dye; her red corduroy shift went ill beneath a shapeless, maroon, knitted cardigan.

At this stage Kristen had spent six weeks in an enclosed convent for wayward girls. This was the last resort of a well-intentioned magistrate who, feeling that she was in need of care and protection, was yet reluctant to commit this 14-year-old to an institution formally constituted to house the State's serious delinquent girls. In that six weeks there had been only two highlights, the first when Kristen decided to escape from the institution, the second, an unscheduled visit to the convent by one of the present writers.

THE FAMILY

General Description

In a sense the house is no different from thousands of others in Melbourne, Australia. It is a relatively new suburb which is already developing pretensions to lower middle class respectability. Essentially a three-bedroom cream brick veneer home, it is of a style which is echoed all around the neighborhood. Externally it is dominated by a drive and terrace area made of dark macadamized stones which crunch uneasily underfoot; the lawn and garden which surround this are moderately well kept, neither being so unkempt as to become a community eyesore nor so neat as to attract envious comment.

Inside it is clean, and predictably though not excitingly or individually furnished. In the lounge a space heater ostentatiously fans hot air onto the clothes airing in the vicinity; the 23-inch television sits like a suburban totem in the corner, enshrined by chairs casually arranged for maximum viewing ease; a set of Reader's Digest encyclopedias graces the solitary bookshelf, proclaiming the family's awareness of the mean by which upward mobility can be achieved. The children's bedrooms, adequately furnished though they are, reflect little of their occupants' personalities, save that of the elder boy whose bedroom door is decorated with a poster which warns: "BEWARE. A SEX MANIAC LIVES HERE." The parental bedroom is dominated by a virginally white nylon bedspread.

It is not a home that would excite comments either of interest or approbation; and yet that home is remarkable for the public face it presents to the secluded court in which it is situated. The front fence is built from 6 foot palings and access can be gained only through two large and solid gates. The venetian blinds are perpetually drawn, the house looks somehow deliberately enshrouded. Seven children and their parents live in that house; only six of those children are allowed to play outside.

Mother:

The mother is a rather drab woman, whose purpose in life derives solely from the security afforded by a continual round of domestic trivia. She is usually fairly conscientious about housework and tends to be compulsively apologetic about a disordered house.

Although only 5 feet 5 inches in height, she seems taller because of the angularity of her bearing and the fact that her clothes tend to hang limply from her frame rather than to complement it. She is always ready to talk and, in fact, is likely to dominate an interview situation by the sheer dispassionate fluency with which she relates incidents and events. Her language is more geared to description than to analysis and she is likely to juxtapose facts, the relationship between which often is highly significant although she herself does not seem to realize it. In our dealings with her she was ever deferential and always appeared ready to answer questions.

Father:

A broad shouldered man, six feet tall and with the ruggedly solid build valued and coveted by so many Australians, the father has a certain presence. Although relatively undereducated, he has been quite successful in business. In recent years he has gravitated from a managerial position in a supermarket chain store to an executive position in the sales division of a welding firm.

In some ways the father is not forthcoming although he

has never been overtly obstructive or unpleasant. Maybe this is because, despite his professional concern with appealing to and interacting with the public, he is a relatively reserved man, disinclined to indulge in discussions of his personal or family life.

Siblings:

Kristen is one of seven children. There is an elder brother, Ian, aged 16, who seemed nervy and insecure until he began working in a local business six months ago. Now he has grown through a sound and trusting relationship with his boss and has an ambition to become a police cadet if he is accepted. Next are non-identical twin girls, Kristen and Pam, age 14. Pam is much smaller than Kristen, slighter in the sense that she lacks Kristen's wiry strength and agility. She is a regular attender at the local church and teaches Sunday school, an activity entirely independent of the rest of the family who do not profess any religion. Although Pam had difficulties of adjustment in early adolescence, she seems much more settled at school now; she had been chosen to represent the school in a basketball competition and she has obtained both a nursing aide and a mothercraft nursing certificate in preparation for a career in nursing. Reg, a boy aged 9; Debbie, a girl aged 7; Bob, a boy aged 3, and Helen at 12 months complete the family.

PERSONAL HISTORY

Early Experience:

Kristen's mother was only 20 when the twins were born. The birth was a normal one and at first the doctor thought that they were identical but, even then, Kristen was much larger than Pam. Her physical development appears to have been normal, perhaps even supernormal, for when at the age of 1 month Kristen had a temper tantrum while her mother was feeding Pam, Kristen thrashed about with such violence that she forcibly propelled herself through the calico end of her bassinet.

This tendency toward displays of aggression and strength continued, for example when Kristen was 7½ months she tipped her twin sister out of her crib. This happened only once because the mother separated the cribs to prevent a recurrence. Kristen at 10 months was able to walk whereas

Pam did not walk until she was 12 months old. Kristen's greater physical mobility enabled her to climb in and out of Pam's cot at will. It was her practice then either to attempt to throw Pam out of the cot or wait until she had finished drinking her bottle and then to break the glass bottle against the side of the cot, showering Pam with broken glass and perhaps cutting her by it.

The mother, at this stage, regarded Kristen as a difficult child, but did not at any time appear to have sought professional advice as to her condition or ways of handling her problem behavior. To some extent this is explicable in terms of the fact that none of the extended family group members gave much credence to the mother's tales of Kristen's exploits. Apparently this pattern was to continue for Kristen showed herself a singular child who tended to evince aggression towards other children and particularly toward cats. The mother reported that at the age of 3 Kristen strangled the cat of the next door neighbor and that since then she had been increasingly violent towards them. She put one cat in a toilet bowl and flushed it and placed another in the washing machine and agitated it. For this reason the family had never had a pet and they have been fearful lest Kristen seize a cat belonging to a neighbor.

Adjustment to School:

Kristen's case was first referred to a school psychologist when she was almost 10 years old and currently attending an outer suburban primary school; even then, in the opinion of the teachers, she was beyond the bound of reasonable discipline. Reports on Kristen's school conduct during the years before referral constantly stressed aggression, wilfullness, and a vindictive disregard both for authority and for classmates.

Earlier, when she was 8 years old, and attending school in a country town, she had exasperated a teacher to the point where he had knocked her down.

Eventually she was transferred from this school to another in the same district because her teacher felt that her conduct was adversely affecting the chances of her brothers and sister, who were also at the school. Even after the transfer, the pattern of aggression and hostility continued. One headmaster commented, in referring Kristen for study by the psychologist, "She has no respect for authority and treats all attempts to reason with her with indifference. The mother has taken her to the police on two occasions in an attempt to prevent her associating with an undesirable character.... In her grade she acts more or less normally, but in the playground she is aggressive and constantly disobeys instructions." Her class teacher at the same school saw her as "a pest who couldn't be trusted, If you turn your back she begins doing something wrong. She is a fluent liar and very vindictive. If a child says something about her she will tear out a page of that child's book. She attacks smaller children, is disliked by other children in the class. The parents are not co-operative although they pretend to be."

This picture of a severely emotionally disturbed child is further compounded by her average IQ range on the WISC. At that time teachers also agreed in describing Kristen as "intellectually capable." She was reading up to grade level, but her math was somewhat retarded—an obvious indication of the impact of emotional problems on her learning progress.

One day when Kristen (aged 11) was absent from school, the class teacher did a sociogram, the results from which are summarized below:

(a) 17 children said that they would not like to have Kristen as a friend;

(b) 18 children said that they would not like to work with her;

(c) no child selected Kristen as a work partner;

(d) no child chose her as a friend;

(e) 21 of the 37 children in the class actively rejected her in one way or another.

At this stage, the pattern of her behavior showed frequent truancy, stealing from neighbors and from school, and malicious "nuisance" telephone calls. Thefts included the stealing of the school stamp. It was her practice then to go around the local neighborhood, and using the school stamp as a symbol of good faith, a confirmation of the validity of her mission, she would "collect" money for the school. Her "nuisance" calls showed an equal inventiveness. "Her star turn," said the headmaster, "was to ring the police one dinner hour. She said she had heard a shot, saw a man run out. She ran in, saw a woman lying dead on the floor. She gave a fictitious address for the police to go to, which they did."

Throughout these years there were marked signs of a growing desperation on all sides. Teachers, policewomen, and psychologists obliged to grapple with Kristen's misdemeanors, a psychiatric center to which she was referred all appeared powerless to arrest the headlong onward course of truancy, malice, and aggression. Her mother made frequent attempts to seek help, pointing out the desperately adverse effects Kristen's conduct was having on the family's image within the neighborhood; but there seemed no way out of the blind alleys of misbehavior. Paradoxically, the mother appeared both to be looking for salvation for her daughter and for punishment. But neither was effectively forthcoming. During this period, too, Kristen moved from primary to secondary school (in her case a single sex school) and reacted to the demands and tensions of this transition by breaking into a house in the neighborhood and stealing a small amount of money. It was less than two dollars, but she was caught, charged, and placed on probation.

Kristen and her father appeared to be opposed to the mother and the other children. The mother surmised that this was because Kristen was so much like her father's side of the family. The home was frequently torn by severe quarrels and arguments, highlighted by incidents of physical violence. The mother lacked the maturity to cope with herself and with Kristen and eventually sought psychiatric assistance on her own account.

Finally, in her second year at high school Kristen was suspended from school for persistent misconduct including assaults on other children and "terrorizing other girls at school and in the neighborhood." Yet interviews with Kristen by school psychologists at this time revealed a picture of a child who saw herself as haunted by diverse fears and demons, as well as aggressions and hatreds. At least some of these expressions of private fears appeared painfully genuine. "I'm just scared to sleep without a light," she said. "I'm scared that somebody's under the bed, somebody's got a gun under the blinds and is going to get through the window. I'm even scared through the day. I'm too scared to sit near the slits of the window in case someone shoots me with a gun. I felt too scared when I was home by myself to have the doors shut. I felt I might want to run out." Conversely, the aggressions continued to show themselves powerfully.

In one interview she said, "I like hurting people. I tell lies about them to other people by using the telephone. I can

Fig. 1.

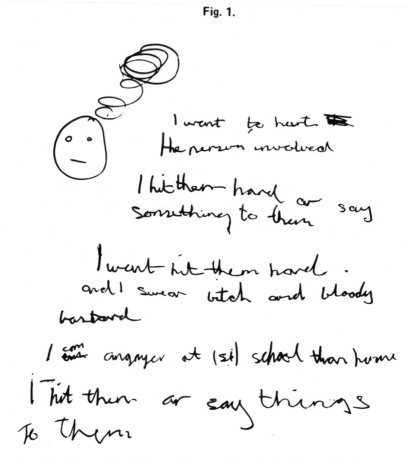

think of horrible things about other girls. They fly into my mind, I feel glad I'm saying them, I want to say them, I can't stop myself from saying them."

AFTER SCHOOL—WHAT?

After Kristen's suspension from school, the psychologist handling her case felt she should not yet return to the normal school but continue education by correspondence, and attend a psychiatric center. Meantime she continued to live at home —and, significantly, interviews from the period reflect a persistent anguish: "Last night I dreamed I was going to die. I couldn't get to sleep. I thought my heart had stopped beating. I asked Pam to choke me." (Fig. 1)

She attended the center (which catered to a few older adolescents and adults up to middle age) from 10:00 a.m. to 4:00 p.m. five days a week, but the pattern of her conduct remained disturbed; in fact, after about eight months, other patients approached the superintendent with what was, in effect, an ultimatum: "Either she goes or we do." She was then transferred to an open residential center for disturbed children; during her six month stay she acted out an almost unceasing pattern of virtually uncontrollable rebellion. One doctor called her "disruptive—in trouble with the supervisors and cruel to the smaller children." She accused one of the nurses of sexual misconduct, but it was later proven beyond doubt that not only was there no substance in this charge but that Kristen herself had been conducting a lesbian relationship with another of the older girls. On some days she ran away four or five times. She was continually telephoning home. She once cut her wrists and at different times took drug overdoses. Within this bleak picture of rebellion however, there remained flashes of the child: she would never run away from the center at night because, she said, she was afraid of the dark.

Finally, in desperation to find a solution, the authorities at the center suggested she be returned home. The center's headmistress wrote: "Her acquired school skills are poor though she is capable intellectually. Most days she will not do anything. Her work output is negligible. I see her as a vicious, cunning, dangerous child. Her nuisance output is tremendous."

At this stage, then, Kristen was catapulted back into her family. While the mother, as aforementioned, clearly had ambivalent attitudes of looking for both help and punishment for Kristen, the father conversely appeared to be going out of his way to fight authority on behalf of his daughter.

Throughout Kristen's school difficulties and periods spent at the psychiatric center and the center for disturbed children, her father's attitude had been one of apparent deep concern and support for his daughter. Even while she was at the residential center, he continually said that he would be happy to have her leave there and return home. The mother, telling of a visit to the residential center with her husband and an interview with a psychiatrist there, said she felt a sense of desperation over the whole situation and felt that her husband was siding with Kristen against her, the mother

—a parental situation in relation to Kristen which had been a marked feature over the years.

Even more stringent measures were taken to hold Kristen within the confines of the home. Since she was so strong and athletic this meant she had to be kept inside the house itself, for once she was outside, she would scale the back fence and be away—either to wreak further mischief or to escape. Hence on her return home, Kristen acted out even more extreme, sometimes bizarre, courses of delinquent behavior. The "nuisance" phone calls to the police began again. After being befriended by a woman neighbor she posed as that neighbor's 4-year-old daughter and telephoned police to accuse the husband of sexual misconduct towards his wife. These calls were so inventively disturbing and vicious that the local police put a detective to tracing them; the detective later admitted to having been surprised that the calls could have come from a teenage girl.

Later Kristen claimed that the woman had told her mother about these phone calls and had misrepresented what Kristen regarded as her way of rescuing the woman from her husband's cruelty. It was this perceived misrepresentation rather than the breach of confidence in itself which motivated Kristen to devise an intricate plan of revenge. She maintained that she had deliberately lost the neighbor's 4-year-old daughter (whose identity Kristen had assumed in making the phone calls) in the local shopping center. Her hope was that the little girl's unusual Christian name would lead the police to identify and investigate the source of the nuisance phone calls.

At about this time Kristen developed a morbid interest in death and the disposal of the dead. Her mother claimed that this appeared at about the same time as a television advertisement extolling the virtues of the service offered by a funeral director. Kristen began to write away for funeral parlor literature and even sneaked herself into the local morgue.

She fought with her sister, and according to her mother, also attempted a lesbian relationship with Pam. The mother became anxious that Kristen did not have enough to occupy her and approached the psychologist in charge of the case with a view to finding some acceptable occupation for her. A job was found for her working at home for a local plastics factory but this lasted no more than two or three days; she abandoned the job and reverted to hours of television view-

Fig. 2

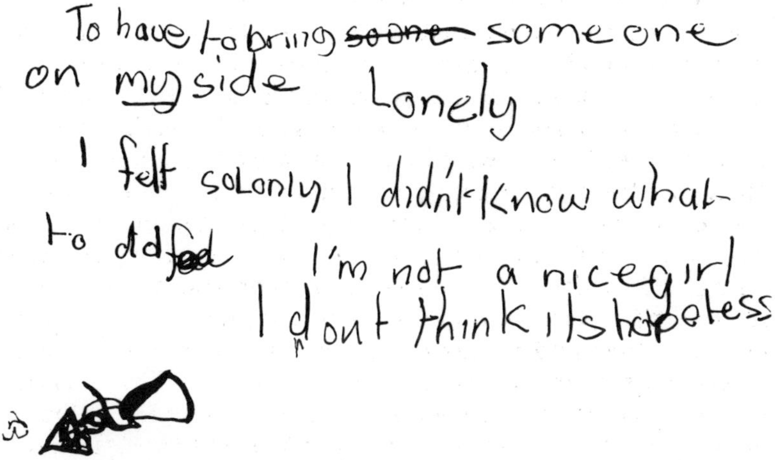

To have to bring ~~some~~ some one
on _my_ side   Lonely
I felt soLonly I didn't know what
to dd~~fed~~   I'm not a nice girl
I dont think its ~~hopeless~~ less

ing, mostly heartbreak, criminal, and personal problem programs. Her aggression within the family did not abate; she even attacked her mother on two occasions—once she had her savagely by the throat against a wall until rescued by the older boy. On the second occasion she was beaten by Kristen with a broom which was snatched away by Father and used to beat Kristen—"one of the few times" (commented the mother) that he had ever inflicted corporal punishment on Kristen. (Fig. 2)

At this stage, the local police called Kristen about her nuisance phone calls. She was, under questioning, defiant and provocative, showing police officers a bottle of sleeping tablets and threatening to take them. She evinced a surprising and highly technical knowledge of sexual practices (deviant and normal) and of drugs, a knowledge so far beyond her years and apparent sophistication that the local police were both educated and shocked. It might be hypothesized that the sole gain to be laid at the door of Kristen's incarceration in the psychiatric center was an induction into the wiles of drugs and their use—hardly an aim of those who had recommended placement there.

The police warned Kristen that her continuing visits to plague them must cease and that her next visit to the police station would be taken as evidence of her being "in need of care and protection" and that she would be made a ward of the State and placed in an institution. A few days after this the mother arrived home from a driving lesson to be met by the neighbor in whose care she had left Kristen because she had felt that the girl was strangely withdrawn and ruminative. Kristen had left and the neighbor had been powerless (or too afraid) to stop her. There was a letter addressed to the mother on the table. It was brief and more "emotional" than anything the mother had ever seen from Kristen:

> Despite what I have done I have always loved you. And I don't think it fair that you should have to put up with what you have to put up with.

The mother was devastated because of the emotional warmth expressed in this note* and was prepared perhaps for something worse than the policeman who finally visited her to say that the police were holding Kristen and removing her to a remand center. Kristen had, in fact, made the decision to give herself up to the police; she was tired of home and its restrictions and she was anxious to remove herself from it. The parents could do no more than acquiesce at this stage and await her appearance before the Children's Court.

When the case was heard, a sympathetic and well-intentioned agency social worker intervened and asked the magistrate for an adjournment so that she could investigate whether there was some alternative to a State detention center for Kristen. This was granted. After a good deal of organizational fracas it was decided that Kristen's best interests would be served by incarcerating her in the half-way house represented by the convent. It was recognized that her chances of future rehabilitation as a citizen might be further reduced if she were placed in a situation of propinquity with girls who had committed more serious offences. The mother's reaction to this, when she talked about it to us, was one of major relief—relief that at least Kristen's problems had been verified as too crippling for the normal family members and environment to handle. She seemed accepting of the fact that Kristen's disturbed behavior patterns might necessitate a lifetime of institutional care.

We felt that the headlong hurl into a confrontation with the law which the growing file on Kristen's case represented was highly disturbing as there seemed no adequate explana-

*In describing this, she claimed that Kristen had not cried until she was 2 years old.

tion of the genesis of Kristen's deviance. Expert opinion agreed that she embodied a problem of considerable magnitude but offered no theory to account for it. There appeared to be no constitutional basis for Kristen's behavior; visibly the family situation was no more stressful or abnormal than Kristen had increasingly caused it to be; her lack of adjustment at school did not seem to be related to any impairment of intellectual functioning. In a sense, then, Kristen's committal to the convent represented almost a last refuge for those who were dealing with the case; it was as if she were being put into cold storage for want of any more purposeful treatment or rehabilitation.

THE DENOUEMENT

Two or three weeks after Kristen was placed in the convent, her problems impinged on us again in a dramatic and unexpected way. Late one afternoon the school psychologist was called to the girl's secondary school which Pam still attended to meet a teacher who had received a note from Pam stating that her father had made sexual advances to her on the previous weekend. Fearful and distraught, she implored the teacher's help and support and admitted her realization that she was a Kristen surrogate. Next morning, confronted with Pam's story, the mother, with the utmost frankness and almost relief, related that Kristen and her father had long been involved in an incestuous relationship and that she had full knowledge of this affair. She had never felt free to venture this information* and always had hoped that one of the people concerned with the case would somehow realize it.

Once the initial recognition was made, the flood gates were opened. According to the mother, the father had first handled both girls sexually when they were no older than 15 months. Although his primary interest had always been in Kristen, at various times over the years he had also undressed Pam and handled her and made her handle him. He had not, however, actually had intercourse with her even on

*She claimed that she had in fact told her psychiatrist who reportedly had responded that she must make the decision either to accept the status quo and to live with it or take steps to effect a permanent separation from the father for herself and the children.

the weekend which precipitated her seeking assistance from the teacher; however, one can surmise that with Kristen gone (possibly for two years) he turned to Pam in lieu of the unavailable Kristen. It became clear that over the years the father consistently had sexual relations with Kristen; he had tampered sexually with his elder son Ian; he had insisted that the twins present themselves for a tactile inspection after they had bathed; he had taken both girls into the parental bed when the mother had been in hospital for the birth of Helen; and his wife had been privy to most, if not all, of this behavior.

These revelations made clear much that hitherto had seemed obscure; a pattern began to emerge. The fact that the mother had had a similar incestuous relationship with her own father, as had her sisters before her, was revealed. Kristen's father, it seemed, had long since been discharged from the army on undisclosed psychiatric grounds. He had a severe alcohol problem and had plummeted the family into considerable debt; Thursday nights were the nights when the whole family sat expectantly on the edge of the paternal volcano. Despite her concern about her husband's alcoholism and the state of the family exchequer, and despite her ambivalence toward Kristen as a sexual rival and as a daughter, the mother had not thought of exposing her husband's deviance to an agency likely to alleviate the situation in any way. There is something masochistic not only in her acquiescence in the situation, but more startlingly in her quite deliberate efforts to shield him.*

Well might Kristen's Grade IV teacher have commented: "The parents are not co-operative although they pretend to be." When Pam's tender-mindedness broke where Kristen's tough-mindedness had remained stalwart under questioning from all manner of skilled counselors, the mother overtly accepted the seriousness of the situation and agreed to talk to the head-mistress at Pam's school and to the chief psychiatrist at a nearby clinic. She flatly refused to lodge any kind of charge against her husband because "I suppose I still love him." The words echoed loudly in the room and then clat-

*For example, when Kristen was placed in the remand center both parents visited her separately and both independently attempted to elicit from her whether she had told the police anything of her sexual involvement with her father.

tered, spent and empty to the floor. Considerable pressure was exerted for both parents to attend the Psychiatric Clinic; they are now both appearing at this clinic—although under sufferance.

Meanwhile Kristen is unhappily at the convent, paradoxically regretful that it was ultimately her own action which took her away from the home situation whose irksomeness and restriction pales by comparison with that of the convent.

She described her day: she rises for mass at 6:00 a.m., has breakfast and works in the convent's industrial laundry from 8:30 a.m. until 5:00 when again she attends prayers, eats the evening meal, watches television for an hour, recites the regulation prayers, and retires to contemplate another such day tomorrow.

She suspects some kind of upheaval took place at home, but has been unable to find out because of the limitations imposed by formal visits. While admitting that she, too, found her father's drinking habits and the Thursday night eruption intolerable, she said, "All of us kids hate it but the others are able to say they hate him. I'm different. I can't." She has no hopes for the future, no sense of a meaningful role in life,* and no means of acquiring either. A pathetic figure, despite her aggressiveness and her sense of revenge, Kristen yet seems to be motivated by a strange kind of integrity, both bizarre and moving. At this stage, the prognosis for Kristen—and possibly her whole family—seems frightening and desperate.

References

Hewitt, L.E., and Jenkins, R.L. (1946). *Fundamental Patterns of Maladjustment: the Dynamics of Their Origin,* Illinois: Michigan Child Guidance Institute.

Jacobson, E. (1957). "Normal and pathological moods: their nature and functions," *The Psychoanalytic Study of the Child,* vol. 12, New York: International Universities Press, 73–113.

Johnson, A.M., and Szurek, S. (1952). "The genesis of antisocial acting out in children and adults," *Psychoanalytic Quarterly, 21,* 323–343.

Kneller, G.F. (1965). *The Art and Science of Creativity,* New York: Holt, Rinehart, and Winston, 28.

Menninger, K., Wayman, M., and Pruyser, P. (1963). *The Vital Balance,* New York: Viking, 200–205.

*She contrasted herself with Pam whom she sees as purposeful and likely to be successful in achieving her ambition to become a nurse.

Shakow, E., and Rapaport, D. (1964). *The Influence of Freud on American Psychology,* New York: International Universities Press.

Related Reading

Bettelheim, B. (1967). *The Empty Fortress,* New York: Macmillan.

Blackham, G.J. (1967). *The Deviant Child in the Classroom,* Belmont, Calif.: Wadsworth.

Buss, A.M. (1961). *The Psychology of Aggression,* New York: Wiley.

Buxbaum, E. (1970). *Troubled Children in a Troubled World,* New York: International Universities press.

Freud, A. (1937). *The Ego and the Mechanisms of Defense,* London: Hogarth.

Schiff, J.L. (1969). "Reparenting schizophrenics," *Transactional Analysis Bulletin, 8* (31), 47–63.

Trilling, L. (1971). "Authenticity and the modern unconsciousness," *Commentary, 52,* 39–50.

Wolff, S. (1969). *Children Under Stress,* London: Allen Lane, Penguin.

Wolman, B.B. (1968). *The Unconscious Mind—The Meaning of Freudian Psychology,* Englewood Cliffs, N.J.: Prentice-Hall.

CHAPTER 6

Susan: A Case of School Refusal

ESTHER MARINE

Editor's Introduction

There always have been some children who refused to go to school. Some have been truants or delinquents; others found school uninteresting or irrelevant so they have chosen life on the street, at work, or in the counter culture. School reluctance is termed school phobia only if there is dread—either dread of separating from home or dread of joining with strangers—and these feelings usually are accompanied by somatic symptoms (Wald-fogel, 1959). The symptoms function to assure that the child will be allowed to remain at, or go, home and they decline as soon as that objective is achieved.

The incidence of school phobia may be more than 1½% of all school aged children and somewhere between 2 and 8 percent of all children referred to clinics (Kahn and Nursten, 1962; Kennedy, 1965). Proportionately higher numbers are reported among the children of professional and managerial parents but this may reflect superior case-finding more than truly different rates.

Broadwin (1932) and numerous writers since have

preferred a psychoanalytic explanation of etiology (Eisenberg, 1958b). School phobia is seen as a deep seated neurosis, a variant of separation anxiety most common in mutually hostile-dependent relations between mother and child. A mother-child symbiosis is often involved. A mother motivated by guilt because she is unable to give generous love becomes overprotective and communicates anxiety about the child's welfare. They signal each other—the child through symptoms, and the mother through over-care. Siblings rarely manifest the same reluctance, but the homes do provide precipitating conditions such as poor fulfillment of mother's emotional needs or temporary threats to the child's security (Estes, Haylet, and Johnson, 1956).

A closely related explanation is that school phobia results when an unrealistic self-image is threatened by school feedback (Radin, 1967). Most vulnerable are children who retain an infantile sense of omnipotence. Their school problem may be aroused on the first day or may wait until some later episode. When the problem manifests late, it has been called "characterological school phobia" and these cases are believed to be more uniformly and deeply disturbed (Coolidge, Hahn and Peck, 1957).

An alternate to analytic explanations is the view that school phobia is maladaptive response or symptom (Goldenberg and Goldenberg, 1970). A school threat initiates flight. Then staying at home is reinforced by avoidance of fear-producing cues at school and by positive reinforcers through the mother's attention and ministrations. Perhaps it is most reinforcing to have mother all to one's self with siblings in school and father at work, or it may simply be reinforcing to interrupt mother's work. Under these conditions the child has little possibility of discriminating between real and imagined dangers.

From either point of view, the current trend is to get the child back to school at once (Weiss and Cain, 1964).

An earlier bias toward slower return with insight before action has given way to the notion that school refusal is an avoidance reaction to a previous stimuli. Staying out, only establishes the symptom and interferes with peer relationships.

Once the child has returned to school, therapy may center on the parents or on the whole family, because there appears to be strong linkage between the phobia and family problems (Waldfogel, Coolidge and Hahn, 1957). The general pattern is to provide for the expression of fear, rage, or guilt, and then help with clarification of these and their relation to school refusal.

A variety of behavioral techniques also have been used. In one case, both classical and operant counter conditioning techniques were used with the conclusion being that the treatment of choice is classical where there are high levels of anxiety and operant in those cases in which avoidance is maintained by secondary reinforcements without fundamental neurotic involvement (Lazarus, Davison and Polefka, 1965). Step-by-step desensitization has been used (Garvey and Hegrenes, 1966) and imposive therapy or the bronco-busting approach has also been tried (Smith and Sharpe, 1970). The repertoire of behavioral technique includes teaching parents so that they become behavioral engineers or managers in the conditioning of a child (Tahmisian and Reynolds, 1971).

Whatever the mode of treatment, the reports are largely positive. Follow-up studies show good success (near 90 percent) in returning young children to school, but much lower success with children over 11 years (Rodriquez, Rodriquez and Eisenberg 1959; Coolidge, Brodie and Feeney, 1964; Weiss and Burke, 1967). While most children return to school, many continue to have significant problems of interrelation. If school phobia is itself symptomatic, the overcoming of the presenting problem may not remove associated deficiencies in the child's behavior. The high efficiency in solving school refusal problems probably reflects the general principle that the most readily promoted behaviors are those that are common, expected, and reinforced in the culture.

PERSPECTIVES ON SUSAN, A SCHOOL PHOBIC

"School refusal" is a relatively common problem of children in our society. It manifests itself in various forms: in the child who refuses to separate from mother and begin school, the student who panics and suffers painful somatic symptoms that render him unable to attend school, and the pupil who finds the teacher or something else in the school situation unpleasant, and therefore, is unwilling to set foot in the school building.

Among the earliest to identify school refusal as an emotional disturbance in certain children were Johnson, Falstein, Szurek, and Sevendsen (1941), a team working in a child psychiatric setting. The investigators noted that many of the children fled from school, and unlike truants, went straight home to mother and refused to return. They were unable to verbalize their fears, and their behavior was incomprehensible to parents and teachers alike. Other reports described cases of school refusal that frequently were accompanied by various types of somatic symptoms (Waldfogel, Coolidge and Hahn, 1957). Their symptoms usually involved the gastro-intestinal tract, but might include other physical symptoms such as aches and pains in the stomach, head, legs, or heart. A common occurrence described in these studies is that of the child who is nauseated and vomiting at breakfast or complaining of abdominal pain. These physical symptoms often do not occur on weekends or during vacation.

Hersov (1960) in a statistical study examined 50 cases of school refusal in a children's department of a psychiatric hospital. He found that persistent nonattenders at school fell into two groups. The children referred for neurotic refusal to go to school came from families with a higher incidence of neurosis. They seemed passive, dependent, and overprotected, yet they exhibited a high standard of work and behavior. The truants, however, came from large families, where home discipline was inconsistent. They had experience of mother's absence during infancy and father's absence during later childhood. They had changed schools often and the standard of work produced by the child was poor.

Eisenberg (1958b) observed the interactions of mothers with their nursery children and noted verbal and nonverbal communications that prevent children from playing with others. Johnson (1957), in an earlier discussion, perceived that the child received the message that the parent wished him to stay at home from school via double talk, oversolicitousness, and numerous unconscious communications. She observed that it is these maneuvers that keep a child immature and regressed. They act as powerful inhibitors and deterrents to maturation and growth.

Talbot (1957) described the inbred characteristics of these families with interdependence between child and mother, and mother and grandmother. Usually the mother feels inadequate in her role and has no outside friends. Johnson, Falstein, Szurek, and Sevendsen (1941, P. 705) stated:

> Study of early life situations of these mothers always show an inadequately resolved dependence relationship to their mothers with intense repressed resentments.

The various case study reports emphasize the mother's preoccupation with her child's welfare, her inability to set limits, and her overprotectiveness which feed his narcissism and omnipotent fantasies. Waldfogel described the mother as being a prisoner of the child, and both mother and child as involved in a hostile relationship (Waldfogel, Coolidge and Hahn, 1957, p. 760):

> These mothers deny hostility by overcompensatory devices and present themselves as being zealously devoted to their child's welfare. They are so terrified of their own angry image, it is hardly any wonder the child shares their fear and needs to protect himself from the full realization of the mother's anger by shifting it to another object. The child must not only deny mother's anger but his own as well.

The fathers of the school-phobic children were not studied until somewhat later. Like the mothers, they too were seen as having a significant role in the pathological constellation: either they were passive, withdrawn, and lacking in responsibility, or they competed with their children. One view was that some fathers, unsure of their sexual indentification, were unable to define a paternal role. Waldfogel, Coolidge and Hahn (1957) thought that some fathers of school-phobic children vie with the mother for the maternal role.

Researchers at the Judge Baker Center, Coolidge, Hahn and Peck (1957) were the first to study "neurotic school phobia".

> The child in the neurotic group displayed acute and dramatic onset of the symptom, often accompanied by clinging behavior which could be more or less persistent . . . The child failed to respond to reasoning or disciplinary measures that in the past parents found effective. In spite of this change, the children continued to function well in all other areas . . . The symptom represents an acute regressive reaction in the face of an exacerbation of a conflict typical for the group. The conflict grows out of the need to establish autonomy in relation to the mother: but on the other hand, implicit in this maturing is the threatening necessity for the child to attempt to resolve his bisexual conflicts . . . These children have attained a primary phallic orientation; it is at this level of psychosexual development that they have blocked. This group of children handles this conflict by the displacement of the focus from mother to school, by a phobic mechanism, and by regressive clinging to the mother. They recognize the undesirability of their new mode of adjustment and wish to master their fears and return to school.

Kennedy (1965) used the dynamic and descriptive data of Coolidge et al. and worked out a differential diagnosis for neurotic school refusal. Seven out of 10 following criteria were needed:

1. Present illness first episode.
2. Monday onset, following illness the previous Thursday or Friday.
3. An acute onset.
4. Lower grades most prevalent.
5. Expressed concern about death.
6. Mother's physical health in question, actually ill or child thinks so.
7. Good communication between parents.
8. Mother and father well adjusted in most areas.
9. Father competitive with mother in household management.
10. Parents achieve understanding of dynamics easily.

TREATMENT PROCEDURES

Treatment for these children has undergone an evolution. An early permissive procedure offered the child who refused to go to school an indefinite medical excuse to stay home, perhaps with a home-bound teacher, while at the same time a psychiatrist and/or social worker tried to help the child and parents resolve the difficulty. Gradually the view emerged that the child's home convalescence reinforced his pathology and made his return to school all the more difficult. This recognition led to setting limits, including insistence on immediate return and concurrent treatment of the child and parents after school hours.

There was agreement in the literature that the onset of school refusal represents a psychiatric emergency; the longer the child stays out of school, the more difficult it becomes to return him, since secondary problems arise due to the loss of academic work and lapsed peer relationships (Talbot, 1957; Waldfogel, Coolidge and Hahn, 1957; Eisenberg, 1958a; Fowlkes, 1963).

Many child guidance clinics now accept this theory and treat such children almost immediately without transferring them to the regular waiting list. The belief has evolved that if treatment of such children is to be effective it must be started promptly and the child returned to school as soon as possible (Finch and Burke, 1960; Bonstedt, Worpell and Lauriat, 1960; Millar, 1961; Buell, 1962). The reasoning behind this procedure is that such action prevents further displacement of fantasied dangers onto the school situation and enables the child to face the reality of his displaced fears much sooner and work out his internal struggle with the conflicting forces of regression and growth.

Kennedy (1965) has described a structured procedure which has been successfully used to return to school those children with mild, neurotic school refusal. He has suggested the following plan of action:

1. Maintenance of good public relations so that doctors, teachers and parents refer cases as soon as possible.

2. Avoid emphasizing the child's inevitable complaints of feeling sick. Parents are instructed to deal with these in a matter-of-fact way of arranging for a medical examination outside school hours.

3. It is essential to be able to require the child to go to school

and to be willing to use any force necessary. Have the father take the child to school. Have the principal or attendance officer take an active part in keeping the child in the room.

4. An interview with the parents in which the therapist is optimistic and outlines a plan of attack. Parents are asked not to discuss the refusal of the child, but simply to announce that the next morning, the child will be returning to school. On the following day the child is dressed and taken to school, regardless of his reaction. In the evening the child must be complimented on staying in school, even if only for 30 minutes and under protest. On the following two days the procedure is repeated. On the evening of the third day, which is usually symptom-free, parents should give a party for the child for overcoming his fear.

5. An interview with the child, always out of school hours, when the therapist relates stories of heroes conquering fear.

6. Follow-up by phone, being chatty, encouraging and not oversolicitous.

Glaser pointed out that one cannot expect such short contact with the child as may be necessary to return him to school to correct basic personality disturbances. However, temporary restoration of emotional balance, the reentry of the child into close contact and relationship with his peers, and the cessation of the pressures and tensions unavoidably occurring when the child portrays such unacceptable behavior as absenteeism from school, may all offer an opportunity for the self-adjusting forces within the child to operate.

In the following pages a case of school refusal will be presented. It demonstrates dramatically the family interaction, the clinical picture of the disturbed child, the approach to diagnosis, and the techniques of treatment.

A CASE OF SCHOOL REFUSAL

The telephone rang at the Child Guidance Center. It was answered by a psychiatric social worker who picked up the intense anxiety and worry in the woman's voice.

"My child Susan, age 9, absolutely refuses to go to school. She has shown reluctance to attend over the past few months, but now she has just stopped going altogether. What should I do?"

"Did you talk to Susan about why she refuses to go?"

"Oh yes. She says she is afraid she is going to be sick. Recently she has refused to go on the school bus, although previously she had traveled this way with her older sister. I did not want to force her so I drove her there myself. She then refused to stay for school lunch; so I picked her up at lunch time and drove her back. Yesterday when I took her to school, she got out of the car, walked to the building and then ran after me, refusing to step inside. This happened a week or so before she complained of stomach pains. At that time, I took her to our family pediatrician and he found nothing wrong. He told me to 'let her take it easy and the problem will go away.' I have tried to take it easy, but Susan is getting worse; she is getting more and more frightened. She tells me that she lies awake at night worrying about school, falling asleep in the early hours. In the morning it is so difficult to make her get out of bed and get ready. It is obvious that she is suffering and I can't bear to see my child this way. It's almost as if school sends her into a panic, because she is fine on weekends and holidays.

"Sometimes I just wonder if I should let her stay home since she is so scared of vomiting and being sick in school. Why, two weeks ago I pushed and got her to school, and do you know, I hardly had arrived back home when the teacher called and told me to pick Susan up; she was nauseous and vomiting."

The social worker took this information and asked, "How does your husband feel about Susan's difficulty?"

"Oh, he's worried too, but you know how it is with men. He is busy with his work and has little time to spend on the family."

"Did you talk to him and let him know you were going to call us?"

"Oh yes. He thought it was a good idea and he said he would be willing to come in with me to see you. You know, I just can't understand it. Susan is such a good child, she does well in school. In fact her teacher told me recently that she always wants to do the perfect job. The other kids like her and the teacher thinks the world of her. He is even willing to come Friday mornings to tutor her specially in the classes she missed. The school has really been very kind. Yesterday the principal saw Susan's panic and she knew how upset I was. She came over to me and suggested I call you. She said she was willing to cooperate in anything you suggested."

The social worker, knowing that school refusal is a symptom of a family crisis and therefore must be treated as soon as possible, made an appointment for both parents to come in the following day.

Mr. and Mrs. James, in their early forties, were a concerned, intelligent couple, the parents of three children. Susan was their youngest and they were completely baffled about how to handle her at this time. During the interview, the mother did most of the talking, although father showed interest and made appropriate comments throughout the session. The parents were supportive of one another and agreed on details of the problem.

Susan had not shown any difficulty previous to last March but there was a serious problem in getting Susan to school from that time until the end of the school year in June. Mrs. James did remember some tears the first week in the first grade, "but that was no real problem." However, an accident involving mother and grandmother had occurred last March. Both women had been shopping, had returned home, parked the car and were on the sidewalk ready to go into the house. A car came careening down the hill, after a 22-month child left in the car had released the brake. Grandmother saw the car, jumped out of the way, but in so doing, fell and suffered a serious fracture of the hip. She was hospitalized and became quite depressed and recuperated slowly. Mrs. James admitted that this was a difficult time for her, and there were still pressures and problems connected with grandmother's stay with the family.

Despite this accident, last summer had been a good one for Susan. She had enjoyed daily visits to the local swimming pool, activities with neighborhood children, and outings planned by the family. Occasionaly she would say, "I hope I don't get sick in the fall. I do so want to start school."

But as soon as school began in September, Susan became more and more apprehensive, forcing mother to drive her to and fro for morning and afternoon sessions. Mrs. James played the role of willing chauffeur, making whatever concessions and sacrifices seemed necessary to make life easier for her child. Yet mother was aware that this was not appropriate behavior for a 9-year-old, that Susan should ride with the others on the school bus, should buy school lunches and should eat in the school cafeteria. She tried to break the pattern by telling Susan that the car would need repairs and that Susan should try again to go with the school bus. Mrs. James was shocked to hear her child's reply.

"Go and borrow grandfather's car or a neighbor's car. I am not going on the school bus and I can't eat in school either."

"All right," mother acquiesced, "if you promise to eat a good lunch, I will pick you up. I don't know how you exist with no breakfast."

Mother realized that Susan was controlling her through her behavior, yet she found it difficult to limit her child. She always felt anxious and insecure when she did not go along with her daughter's requests.

Mrs. James sympathized with her daughter and believed she knew just how Susan felt. "You know," she commented to the social worker, "I felt like Susan a few years ago when I was really depressed." Father added that at that time he was busy with his work and commitments and was not too helpful. However, mother was able to talk to her family doctor, who prescribed medication. Gradually the depression lifted. Last year, however, she experienced symptoms of extreme hunger, dizziness, and weakness. She learned that she had a "slight case of sugar diabetes."

Susan at that time expressed concern about her mother. She mentioned to father that she was worried about what would happen to mother. Her fears of losing mother made her appear almost like an infant.

Both parents fondly remember Susan's infancy. They agreed they enjoyed this child more than the first two.

"Her delivery was easy," stated mother. "She went through the usual stages without incident. She started school in the first grade because there was no kindergarten in the community. She has always been a very good student. It is such a shame that this has happened. She may be a bit shy but she has friends. We are *very* anxious to have your help."

"Perhaps we have been too lenient with her. We have not expected as much from her as we should." commented the father.

Both parents agreed to continue their efforts to get Susan to school regularly. It was suggested that Susan stay in school for lunch, because of the increased pressure of coming home and then again returning to school. An appointment was made for the following week with the recommendation that the family should call if they needed help in the meantime.

The next day mother called, quite upset.

"It is just impossible with Susan. I was not able to get her to stay in school today. I took her this morning, but she became hysterical, and I brought her home. She threatened to kill herself, but I told her, "You might not die, you might cripple yourself." "You would want me dead even more," Susan yelled back."

The social worker suggested the following reply for mother. "Daddy and I don't want you to harm yourself and we won't let it happen, but it's a girl's job to go to school, and we are going to help you do this. I know it's hard now, but it won't be for long."

It was significant that although Susan was to treat the other children to cookies, she could not bring herself to stay in school. Mrs. James responded to her daughter's hysterical outburst and gave in. Susan came home and settled down to enjoying herself reading her favorite magazine. Her mother was not too worried about school work since Susan's latest report card showed good grades despite absences. The work was made up by special tutoring each Friday evening.

At the next session the social worker gave direct advice to parents, telling them bluntly that Susan had to go back to school and stay the entire day. Susan was not to come home for lunch and mother was not to show concern about how much Susan ate. The parents were prepared for their daughter's negative behavior. The school was also called and prepared for possible hysterical reaction by Susan.

The following morning Susan was taken to school by father. She was quite emotional before leaving the house. With great difficulty, mother got her to dress. She would put clothes on and take them off, crying all the while. After she was settled in the car, Mrs. James handed her the lunch.

The teacher commented later that Susan whimpered a few times during the day, but he reassured her and asked her to sit down. Susan followed his orders and participated well. However, she refused to go to the lunch room and sat by herself in the classroom eating alone. Several times Susan went to the school secretary, saying she was ill and needed to go home. The secretary had been informed of the treatment plan and cooperated by saying, "You look okay to me; go back to your class." Susan complied.

Since then, Susan has attended school each day with lessening anxiety. She felt a little anxious before leaving home with father, but sitting a few minutes reading a book calmed her down. The following week, father brought Susan after school to see the social worker.

SUSAN AND THE SOCIAL WORKER

Susan was a tall, thin, rather frail looking attractive child. She was neatly dressed in a Black Watch plaid jumper, white blouse, and knee socks. Her hair was cut short in a pixie. Facially she resembled her mother. When she was first noticed in the waiting room, she was absentmindedly wringing her hands. After father's introduction, she looked at him, then grinned at the clinician and separated easily to go for her interview. She followed quickly and walked with a certain ease and grace.

The clinician described the procedure in the playroom and suggested that Susan could choose the toys she wished to use. The child walked over to a table with two chairs and sat down facing the mirror. The social worker sat down too; Susan avoided looking at her directly but she did watch the reflections in the one-way mirror.

Susan was cooperative. She had a need to please adults, but she was extremely anxious, avoiding eye contact, rubbing her hands, and pulling her socks. She relaxed when Tip-It, a balancing game, was introduced. She played according to the rules, won and lost a game. She found it difficult to say much about her problem this first time but admitted being anxious about coming to the center, although her parents had told her about the purpose of her visit. "I know I am coming here because I am afraid to go to school. I am afraid I may get sick. I used to be afraid my mother would get hurt while I was away but I haven't thought about that too much since I started back to school.

"I don't want to be afraid; I want to go to school like the other kids, and my mother said you could help me. I get most nervous in the morning before I leave the house. I wish I could quit worrying about going to school."

Although a dish of candy was on the table during the session and although Susan was offered some M&M's, she refused to take any until the end of the hour when she was offered some again. Then she took one piece and thanked the social worker.

The second session saw a more relaxed child, who talked

more easily, smiled more readily and even joked about not facing the therapist. A variety of puppets had been placed on the table before Susan arrived. While giving pertinent information about herself and the family, she began fingering the puppets. After awhile she would stand them up and knock them down repeatedly and squeeze their faces to distortion. Finally she picked up the baby puppet and suggested she would be the baby and the social worker the mother. They role played going to the store and buying candy. Susan then played a family scene showing who liked whom.

"Mother likes daddy because he buys her things; mother likes grandma because she baby-sits; mother likes sister because she helps with the dishes. Mother likes brother because he is good looking. Father likes mother because she is good looking. Father likes grandma because she buys the kids things when he can't. Father likes sister because she helps mother. Father likes brother because he has lots of girlfriends."

"What would the people change about each other?" asked the therapist.

Mother wanted Dad to quit smoking. Father wanted mother to make better spaghetti; father wished grandma would not act like a baby; sister did not like brother's boyfriends, and her parents wanted Susan to go to school. And so the hour ended and the evaluation was completed.

The therapist recognized that Susan was unable to express angry feelings, especially to her mother. There was a suggestion of a slight symbiotic relationship between mother and child which was arousing a great deal of hostility in Susan. She was defending against these feelings by projecting her anxiety onto the school situation. The parents had handled the school refusal previously by inconsistency and they had difficulty with, and guilt about separation. With professional help the parents were able to insist on regular attendance. The school was supportive in helping Susan remain in class and the building.

This case was brought to a staff meeting with a child psychiatrist acting as chairman. Questions were raised about father's role in the family and mother's feelings regarding the children growing up and leaving her. The themes of injury and preoccupation with eating were noted.

The clinical impressions were accepted and the diagnosis of psychoneurotic disorder, phobic type, was agreed upon.

It was recommended that Susan be seen for short term treatment of one hour a week for three months. Her parents would be concurrently helped. The treatment goals for Susan were:

(1) help her eat in the cafeteria with the other children,

(2) help her participate with other children during recess,

(3) help her go by school bus,

(4) help her be unafraid when going to the school office for supplies.

Play therapy was the treatment technique used to enable Susan to play out, act out and talk out her feelings in relation to the family and school.

The goals for the parents were:

(1) to help mother separate from Susan in order to establish more autonomy for the child;

(2) to help father become more involved with mother and the children;

(3) to help mother get more involved in activities outside the home and permit Susan to grow up.

Work with the parents was focused mainly on feelings regarding Susan's growing up and breaking away from the family. Advice and guidance was given around concrete problems involving Susan's functioning in school. Educational techniques were used to explain separation anxiety related to the youngest child growing up. Mother was encouraged to obtain part-time work and become involved in activities outside the home.

In the three month period, Susan continued to improve. She was well motivated and wanted to please. She soon discovered that she was not afraid of the cafeteria at all and began to eat her lunch there. After this occurrence she became more confident in her ability to overcome obstacles and was able to go to the office for paper and become more active with other children during recess. She functioned well in school for the rest of the year.

The parents were basically healthy and well-motivated people. They followed through effectively on all suggestions. Father became more involved with mother and the children. Mother found a part-time job as a sales clerk in a local store and joined a church organization. This left less time to spend with Susan, the symbiotic relationship was weakened. Susan began to grow up.

Although occasionally Susan reverted to infantile behavior, mother and father were able to handle this regression by planned ignoring and giving positive reinforcement to mature, age-appropriate behavior. Previously, she had required mother to sit with her while she did her homework. Later, Mrs. James did not stay in the room, but made herself available when asked directly for help. Previously, Susan was anxious when parents went dancing on Saturday night, trying to hold them by continuous questioning—Where are you going? When will you be home? Later, she accepted the fact that parents went out and returned.

DISCUSSION

The above case illustrates the panic and crisis of the whole family involved with a child experiencing acute neurotic school refusal. A sense of impotence on the part of parents coupled with sympathy on the part of school personnel created a situation in which school refusal was supported. Crisis intervention by any mental health casetaker clinician has been proved to be effective with these problem children. Marine (1966) showed that there was no significant difference between intervention by an untrained home and school visitor or by a professional staff member of a child guidance clinic.

The Kennedy model was significantly helpful in making the diagnosis of acute, mild, neurotic school refusal for Susan James. It separated her difficulty from the severe chronic school refusal situation. Susan James' problem was categorized mild acute school refusal because:

(1) It was an acute onset.

(2) She was in the lower grades.

(3) There was expressed concern about death.

(4) Mother's physical health was in question (diabetes) and child knew it.

(5) There was good communication between parents.

(6) Mother and father were well adjusted in most areas.

(7) Parents achieved understanding of dynamics easily.

Kennedy (1965) reportedly achieved 100 percent success for 50 treated cases using his structured treatment cure cited previously. Marine's typology (1968–69) of school refusal enabled appropriate method of treatment to be selected easily.

References

Bonstedt, T., Worpell, D., and Lauriat, K. (1962). "Difficulties in treatment of school phobia," *Diseases of the Nervous System, 23,* 75–83.

Broadwin, T.A.A. (1932). "A contribution to the study of truancy," *American Journal of Orthopsychiatry, 2,* 253.

Buell, F.A. (1962). "School phobia," *Diseases of the Nervous System, 23,* 79–84.

Coolidge, J.C. Hahn, P.B., and Peck, A.L. (1957). "School phobia: neurotic crisis or way of life," *American Journal of Orthopsychiatry, 27,* 296–306.

Coolidge, J.C., Brodie, R.D., and Feeney, B. (1964). "A ten-year follow up study of 66 school phobic children," *American Journal of Orthopsychiatry, 34,* 675–695.

Eisenberg, L. (1958a). "School phobia: a study in the communication of anxiety," *American Journal of Psychiatry, 114,* 712–718.

Eisenberg, L. (1958b). "School phobia: diagnosis, genesis, and clinical management," *Pediatric Clinics of North America, 5,* 645–666.

Estes, H.R., Haylet, C.H., and Johnson, E.M. (1956). "Separation anxiety," *American Journal of Psychiatry, 10,* 682–695.

Finch, S.M., and Burke, H.L. (1960). "Early psychotherapeutic management of the school phobia," *Post-Graduate Medicine, 27,* 140–147.

Fowlkes, N.P. (1963). "A follow-up study of school phobia case," *Smith College Studies in Social Work, 34,* 50–51.

Garvey, W., and Hegrenes, S.R. (1966). "Desensitization techniques in the treatment of school phobia," *American Journal of Orthopsychiatry, 36,* 147–152.

Glaser, K. (1959). Problems in school attendance: school phobia and related conditions, *Pediatrics, 55,* 758.

Goldenberg, H., and Goldenberg, I. (1970). "School phobia: Childhood neurosis or learned maladaptive behavior," *Exceptional Children, 37,* 220–226.

Hersov, L.A. (1960). "Persistent non-attendance at school: Refusal to go to school," *Journal of Child Psychology and Psychiatry and Allied Disciplines, 1,* 130–145.

Johnson, A.M. (1957). "School phobia," *American Journal of Orthopsychiatry, 27,* 307–309.

Johnson, A.M., Falstein, E.I., Szurek, S.A., and Sevendsen, M. (1941). "School phobia," *American Journal of Orthopsychiatry, 11,* 702–711.

Kahn, J.H., and Nursten, J.P. (1962). "School refusal: A comprehensive view of school phobia and other failures of attendance," *American Journal of Orthopsychiatry, 32,* 707–718.

Kennedy, W. (1965). "School phobia; Rapid treatment of fifty cases," *Journal of Abnormal Psychology, 7,* 285–289.

Lazarus, A.A., Davison, G.C., and Polefka, D.A. (1965). "Classical and operant factors in the treatment of school phobia," *Journal of Abnormal Psychology, 70,* 225–229.

Marine, E. (1968–69). "School refusal—who should intervene?" *Journal of School Psychology, 7,* 63–70.

Marine, E. (1966). "School refusal treatment in two agencies: A followup study of intervention by a child guidance center and an attendance and counseling division of a school system," unpublished doctoral dissertation, University of Pittsburgh, Pittsburg, Pa.

Millar, T.P. (1961). "The child who refused to attend school," *American Journal of Psychiatry, 118,* 390–404.

Radin, S.S. (1967). "Psychodynamic aspects of school phobia," *Comprehensive Psychiatry, 8,* 119–128.

Rodriguez, A., Rodriguez, M., and Eisenberg, L. (1959). "The outcome of school phobia: a follow up based on 41 cases," *American Journal of Psychiatry, 116,* 540–544.

Smith, R.E., and Sharpe, M. (1970). "Treatment of school phobia with implosive therapy," *Journal of Consulting and Clinical Psychology, 35,* 239–243.

Tahmisian, J.A. and Reynolds, W.T. (1971). "Use of parents as behavioral engineers in the treatment of a school-phobic girl," *Journal of Counseling Psychology, 18,* 225–228.

Talbot, M. (1957). "Panic in school phobia," *American Journal of Orthopsychiatry, 27,* 286–295.

Waldfogel, S. (1959). "Emotional crisis in children," in H. Burton (Ed.), *Case Studies in Counseling and Psychotherapy,* Englewood Cliffs, N.J.: Prentice Hall.

Waldfogel, S., Coolidge, J.C., and Hahn, P.B. (1957). "The development, meaning and management of school phobia," *American Journal of Orthopsychiatry, 27,* 754–780.

Weiss, M., and Cain, B. (1964). "The residential treatment of children and adolescents with school phobia," *American Journal of Orthopsychiatry, 38,* 294–295.

Weiss, M., and Burke, A.G. (1967). "A five to ten year follow up of hospitalized school phobic children and adolescents," *American Journal of Orthopsychiatry, 38,* 294–295.

Related Reading

Berecz, J. M. (1968). "Phobias of childhood: etiology and treatment," *Psychological Bulletin, 70,* 694–720.

Marine, E. (1968). "1968 school refusal: review of the literature," *Social Service Review, 42* (4), 464–478.

Nice, R.W. (1968). "The use of sodium, etc.," *Journal of Learning Disabilities, 2, 249–255.*

Patterson, G.A. (1965). A learning theory approach to the problem of the school phobic child," in L. P. Ullman and L. Kasner (Eds.), *Case Studies in Behavior Modification, New York: Holt, Rinehart and Winston,* 279–285.

Rabiner, C. (1969). "Impramine treatment of school phobia," *Comprehensive Psychology, 5,* 387–390.

CHAPTER 7

Helen: A Case of Anorexia Nervosa

JEAN D. WICKLUND

Editor's Introduction

This case illustrates major factors seen in classic cases of anorexia nervosa. Typically, the patient is a female in the mid-teens or early twenties who exhibits a history of success in school and personal relations. As starvation proceeds, such physiological changes as amenorrhea and extreme emaciation ensue. Anorexia is considered a *symptom,* often set off by some traumatic early experience in which food played a prominent role. In this instance, it may relate to problems in feeding such a small child or finding an appropriate milk-substitute, along with concomitant parental anxiety.

Eating, or declining to eat, may be part of a power struggle between parent and child—in this case, between Helen and her mother. Mother exercised power in moving the younger sister out of Helen's room and may have instigated a clash. This was exacerbated by Helen's lack of preparation for the physical changes attending puberty and her ambivalence about her emerging sexuality. The resistance to growing up and the unrealistic vacillation between seeking contacts with boys and then failing to follow through is closely related to the restriction on growth and the flattening of body contours to prepubertal dimensions through extreme fasting.

Typically Helen showed hostility toward family and physicians as they sought to intervene to preserve her health. She was also typical in fluctuating between obesity and starvation, both at the beginning of the sequence, and later even after several years of therapy. Typical also was the attempt to live out most of her conflicts in the single symptom of self-starvation. Only when she began to gain insight into her ambivalence about growing up and into her anger at her mother's rejection and tight control was Helen able to stabilize her weight and move toward womanhood.

BACKGROUND—CASE OF HELEN

Refusal to eat in an adolescent child has been a familiar medical syndrome for centuries. In 1694 Richard Morton described two cases, a boy and a girl. He thought the problem stemmed from "sadness and anxious cares." The description of the girl is dramatic and characteristic of all cases presented through the years. At one point he states that she was "like a skeleton clad only with skin." The girl in the present study had not reached such a point of emaciation and did not die as did the early case. However her apparent need to starve herself is classic.

The syndrome typically arises at the age of puberty or shortly after, and is more common in girls than boys. The most obvious sympton is a determined refusal to eat which leads to thinness and wasting. Related symptoms often described are chronic constipation, the abrupt cessation of menses, and overactivity or denial of fatigue.

There appear to be two forms of anorexia. One is characterized by severe neurotic or schizophrenic conflict, while the other, true anorexia nervosa, is marked by disturbances of body image of delusional proportions. Hilda Bruch (1965) states that the child victim often has experienced a long-standing sense of personal ineffectiveness, especially in relation to mother and a resulting "deficit in confirmation of child-initiated behavior."

Helen's Family

Helen Moore was the first grandchild for both sides of her family. Her birthdays had been occasions for large family gatherings and her achievements were strongly anticipated.

Mrs. Moore was large, heavy, plainly but nicely dressed, and somber faced. Helen described her as "great fun, a person who sacrifices for her children" but I remember her as one who denied any difficulties with Helen, who tended to deny the existence of ward rules, and who was an obstructionist toward psychiatric treatment of her daughter. On almost every visit she asked me if I had yet found the physical cause for her daughter's illness and inquired when she would be allowed to take Helen home.

On the eve of Helen's thirteenth birthday, mother became quite angry with me when, on both emotional and physical grounds, I refused permission for a large family birthday party. Helen's weight was at the low point of her illness and the last thing she needed was to have relatives peering at the thin, pitiful creature she had become. Her mother was hostile, insisted this was an important birthday which should be spent at a party at home. She told me that I had been dishonest in stating that I would look after her daughter's emotional welfare.

Helen appeared quite content in observing or provoking disagreement between Mrs. Moore and myself. While her mother insisted on a pass to go home, Helen appeared disinterested and in fact did not request the pass.

Helen described her father as being "fine, but he can be serious too; he's a good father." He was tall, somewhat thinner than his wife, well dressed and good looking. He was concerned about his daughter and eager to go along with the prescribed treatment. However, his understanding was intellectualized and he did not focus attention on the immediate needs of the child. He frequently spent his visits walking arm-in-arm with Helen around the hospital ward.

Helen's youngest sister was her favorite in the family. Mr. Moore stated that Helen was very reliable and had taken good care of her little sister. She was a pretty, sparkly eyed little girl who enjoyed being the center of attention. She rarely spoke out in the family sessions but captivated attention by giggling, wiggling, looking at Helen, or poking her mother. Her typical response to questions was the same as that of other children—a long questioning look toward mother. Mother then explained that the child had not understood the question.

Helen shared a room with this sister until house remodeling began, about six months prior to the hospital experience. Though Helen's imminent puberty may have prompted the parents' decision to provide Helen a room of her own, the stated reason was that her younger sister had been the one to request a separate room. It did not appear to have been Helen's choice.

Early Development

Helen was the product of a difficult pregnancy. Her mother had suffered severe toxemia and was bed-ridden for several weeks prior to the induction of labor at eight months. Helen stayed in an incubator for several weeks until her weight increased to five pounds and she was strong enough to go home.

Helen's father reported that it had been difficult to handle and feed such a "bird like thing" for the first six months. The mother said "she had lots of gas and constipation," various milks were tried and the eventual choice was a soybean product.

By nine months, Helen was taking most foods. It was at this time the family moved to a house next door to and owned by the grandparents Moore. It was apparently a gift to the younger family. Though at first the parents denied any continuing problems with Helen, they mentioned that she sucked her thumb until age 6, appeared to have a continually clogged nose, chapped lips, and chronic constipation. She preferred her hair long and cried furiously whenever it was cut.

ONSET

Seven months prior to hospitalization, Helen appeared to be happy, pleasant and agreeable, a 12-year-old doing B and

C work in school. Her main interests were Campfire Girls, a folk music group, and intramural sports. She had "dropped one girl friend who had begun to wear make up and talk about boys."

About this time, Mrs. Moore noted the onset of menses and Helen's "breasts flopping" under her sweat shirt during volley ball. She informed Helen that she would have to begin wearing a bra. I asked Helen's mother how she had approached discussing puberty and was told that she herself had been sent to the family doctor, but that Helen had seen films at Campfire Girls. She dodged the issue of discussion with Helen herself.

Several months later Helen was noted to be a bit chunky on a routine physical examination for camp. Helen remembered that her pediatrician had indicated that she was a bit overweight but Helen was not concerned at the time. She went to camp and then spent the rest of the summer next door with grandmother, snacking on pop and cookies.

The motivation to diet began with shopping for school clothes. There were no clothes in the girls' section in sizes that would fit. Helen decided to cut down on food and soon was not only cutting down on snacks but on her portions of food at mealtime. For several months both Helen and her family were pleased with the results of her weight loss. Her parents became concerned in December when they noted that she was taking food portions "so small, they were ridiculous." By Christmas Helen's weight had dropped to about 100 pounds. She later told me that she then "felt so good" that she decided to cut down to water only. She remembered "feeling strong and enjoying daily exercising."

Around the first of the year, Helen's parents took her to the pediatrician. She was given tests and placed on a routine of weekly vitamin shots with other preparations to help her gain weight. The parents report a dramatic personality change with Helen becoming irritable. She requested her family and her physician to leave her alone.

Helen recalled those days as a struggle between herself and her parents. She wondered why they did not understand the great feat she had accomplished in losing so much weight, and her fears of "getting fat." She was hungry and wanted food, but was frightened that eating would make her "cells swell up." I asked her where and she pointed to her hips and thighs.

HOSPITALIZATION

Helen was admitted to the general pediatric ward in February at a weight of 86 pounds. Again a number of tests were done to find any physical basis for Helen's anorexia and weight loss. After a week of extensive examinations, continued anorexia and weight loss, the consensus was that a physical basis for Helen's illness could not be found. She was referred for psychiatric consultation and soon transferred to a psychiatric ward.

When I (her therapist) first met her, she was tearful, anxious, and appeared severely depressed. She was in skirt, blouse, and knee socks and had very long, straight, brown hair. She was shy but warm, and while we talked she often stared into space.

Occasionaly in answer to a question, she would look at me, smile broadly and answer "Yeh." She appeared unable to volunteer information about herself or her thoughts on dieting. She told me that she just wanted to go home and "be happy again."

She frequently cried during sessions and her face was perpetually red and tearful. She used reams of tissues, dabbing her eyes, nose, and spitting out excess saliva.

Helen was told that she had a psychiatric illness and that it was one in which we would need her full cooperation. Both she and her parents expressed fear and resistance to the idea of psychiatric illness. Indeed it was my impression that the parents *never* completely accepted the fact that there was no physical basis for Helen's anorexia.

It was a struggle to work at understanding Helen's side of the problem while firming up a contract with her to eat enough to sustain life. A child who would not eat also generated anxiety in the ward staff. To the pressure from Mrs. Moore was added that of nurses and other psychiatrists who wished for some magic that would make Helen eat—or they wanted me to force feed her. I felt that Helen should develop anxiety about her state of health plus build trust that would enable her to overcome her fears. However, she continued to be unable to follow any diet plans set up for her or set up by herself. After a month of steady weight loss, I put Helen on supplemental Sustagen feeding (a high protein milk shake) each evening.

After four days of these feedings, Helen asked to try again

the regular meals without the threat of having to drink this rather unpalatable milkshake. She agreed that if her weight fell below 70 pounds we would have to set up a regular supplemental feeding plan. She accepted that I could not risk her health and possibly even her life just because of her overwhelming fears of food and "being fat."

Soon after admission to the psychiatric ward, I requested psychological testing. The examiner observed a "very thin, sallow, acutely uncomfortable girl who gave test associations reluctantly and hesitantly, sometimes swallowing her words." When asked to repeat, she often used different sounding words.

She seemed to set herself the task of telling happy stories with "everything turning out all right in the end." For example, in one story in the *TAT* she had said that a wife figure had become ill and died but she ended this story, "But suddenly one day, she suddenly starts to get better and it turns out she gets well again."

On the *Rorschach,* Helen produced limited and highly guarded responses. She used only the most obvious "safe" precepts. She was reluctant or unable to trust the examiner with any more intimate exploration of her feelings. She told me that she could never be angry with her parents because they were "so nice all of the time." She appeared to see no inconsistency between "never being angry" with them while refusing to eat the food that her mother carefully prepared and desperately wanted her to have.

Following the contract for Helen to manage her own diet and yet limit her weight loss, she became warmer and closer to me. She said that she was pleased that I had confidence in her and trusted her to try hard to eat again. Over the next few weeks, she tried. She was frequently tearful though attempting to appear physically active and happy.

Her strength was diminishing and her speech became soft and nearly monosyllabic. Often she begged for passes to go home where, she claimed, she would eat. However, when she returned to the hospital, she would complain that the weekend visit had been too short and that she had been forced to come back "home," meaning the hospital, too soon.

In ensuing weeks, Helen ate irregularly. She frequently came to my office and cried, stating that she had only wanted to lose weight in the beginning to feel better and now things were "quite a mess." Finally Helen went below 70 pounds.

This time, she anticipated that she would have to begin supplemental feedings. She told the nurse who weighed her that she was disappointed about her weight, but relieved when the decision was made to take over feeding her, and thus take the pressure off mealtime.

I gave Helen somewhat more palatable milkshakes during hours not associated with mealtimes, mid-morning, mid-afternoon, and late evening. I felt it necessary to keep mealtimes undisturbed and place the Sustagen in the realm of a medication. I took the first feeding to Helen myself. She drank it quickly and handed me back the container. In the evening she drank the Sustagen in front of her mother with dramatic effects. Mother was seen leaving the ward in tears, too upset to attend a parents' meeting scheduled for that evening.

Helen denied anger toward her mother, but the anger in this act is obvious by its results. Mother had failed in efforts to feed her child, and now another person was feeding her. She must have been furious.

The next day I sat with Helen as she was picking at the breakfast tray. She complained that she hated mealtimes because she was watched so closely by the nurses. I observed that she really had eaten very little and this made them worry. She verified my observation of her tray and proceeded to eat over half of what was left.

The battle about eating appeared to be over. Helen's weight increased steadily. Helen frequently expressed to staff the wish to please me and appeared to equate eating and drinking and supplemental feedings with earning favor and gaining passes out of the hospital. She became tearful in her sessions with me and began opening up some of her ideas and fantasies.

Three days after beginning the Sustagen feedings on a regular basis, Helen became age 13. She informed the staff that now she was a "teen-ager." She implied that she had had some fears about her approaching birthday. She stated that she felt that people grew up at their own pace and not by chronological age. She was unable to elaborate further except to say that she was glad that she had not "changed in any way by becoming a teen-ager."

A few days later Helen told her nurse that she was hungry when her hospital tray was late. She began to relax with other teen-agers on the hospital ward and appeared to enjoy attending activities with them. She continued to gain weight over several weeks and was discharged nearly four months after admission with weight back up to 100 pounds.

CLINICAL FOLLOW-UP

Stage I

Helen returned to the clinic weekly for the next year. She used me much as a younger sister would talk to an older one. She related her week's activities and events in a superficial but friendly manner. My comments were taken with a quiet, thoughtful expression on her face. At times I attempted to explore deeper feelings in the realms of identification and sexuality, but she usually only listened and was unable to contribute.

Her weight stabilized at 120 pounds—slightly heavy for her—but attractive. Refusal to eat never again became a real problem. On Helen's first visit back after hospital discharge she brightly concluded, "Everything is just great." Later, she sobered a bit and said, "I keep thinking how dumb I was— not eating." She confessed that she still had occasional urges to diet, especially when she wore her cut-off shorts taking walks with her father. She felt that her shorts were too tight, but added that she knew she was still quite thin.

Now it may be useful to draw together some related dynamics, including the fact of Helen's mother telling her that she "flopped too much." Helen claimed she, herself, was unaware of this. Then her "little" sister was moved out of her room and constant care. Father was concerned and perhaps overly seductive in his behavior toward Helen. Mother was hostile, rejecting and yet dominating. Helen must cope with her own individuality and the problems associated with puberty while experiencing fairly insensitive behaviors on the part of her parents. She renounced womanhood, starved herself, and continued to feel the need to starve herself whenever normal sexual feelings were aroused by father.

Helen's feelings might also be conceptualized as rising from a wish to have a baby—perhaps father's baby. With puberty coming on, rejection by mother, less sharing with little sister, going to Grandmother's to talk and eat cookies and pop, she renounced all of these feelings and starved herself. Most of this can be but conjecture, since Helen was unable to relate more than superficial associations in this phase of the treatment. She tended to deny stressful or unpleasant feelings and wished to view her world as that of a consistently "happy family."

Helen began taking baby-sitting jobs and took up again with Campfire Girls and her school chums. Just before school opening she came to our session sporting a short hair cut. I asked her about her previous fears when having her hair cut and she denied them. (Since I had received this information from mother, I am not sure whether this was Helen's denial of problems or mother's delusion.)

I did not let Helen completely avoid her anxieties about her family and her eating. She noted the urge to eat was strongest when she and mother were alone together in late afternoon. The other siblings usually were out playing. She related this to feeling anxious and the next urge was to try to avoid eating. She soon found that spending more time away from home decreased the anxiety. I dubbed her former need to starve herself a "delusion" and we used this term in discussing this urge.

At times I related some of her feelings to her physical maturation and the drives that accompany puberty. Helen stated flatly that she had seen films about this in Campfire Girls and did not wish to discuss it further.

Nearly a year from the time Helen had begun her strict dieting she indicated a first interest in boys. She came in and seemed particularly pleased to tell me about a boy she liked who "goofed off in art class." She presented herself as a mildly mischievious person with a sense of humor and bubbly personality. She behaved much differently in her sessions now. She was no longer thin and weepy. She was instead a slightly unkempt preadolescent, not pretty, but not unattractive.

When Helen stabilized her diet and social life and felt little need to explore deeper aspects of her illness, we began to talk of termination. She chose the pattern of declining frequency of visits and I followed her lead.

I again requested psychological testing a few months before termination. The psychologist concluded that Helen displays considerable restriction in her feelings and has a "classical defense makeup." In spite of some indications of anxiety about sexual identification and body structure, she appears to be functioning well. There are indications of a relative inability to handle demands for close, affective involvement, along with indications that she considers her own emotional makeup to be foreign and beyond her control. Helen's visits tapered off and termination was matter of fact.

Stage II

Helen accomplished most of her growth during this "stage" by herself. Nearly a year and a half after termination, she called and asked to see me again. She had changed dramatically. She was an attractive 16½-year-old girl, wearing make up, long hair, simple, but nice clothing, and nylons.

This year and a half was part of therapy because Helen told me that she frequently had recalled our discussions. She developed a mode of operation by figuring out what "her lady would say about it."

She now was stumped on a problem and felt that I might be able to help. She began by telling me that her weight had fluctuated, and at one point was up to 160 pounds. She now was back to 120. Her main concern was a feeling of loss and depression. She explained that she and her girl friend had become quite obsessed with thinking about a particular folk group. They had collected pictures, records, and a great deal of fan material about them. Each had picked out a member of the group as a "boy friend."

This was when Helen began caring more about dress and makeup. In anticipation of going to California and meeting the folk group on their home ground, Helen had begun to make herself attractive. She openly told me that she had fully expected to be welcomed lovingly and warmly when she arrived. However, the trip turned out to be a great disappointment. She was not even recognized, much less welcomed. Helen came back disillusioned and depressed. She determined to, and did, put away her records and fan material. Now, two months later, she felt anxious and depressed.

We discussed the fact that she had needed a fantasy boy friend in order to mature her femininity and reach some separation from her family. Her family, incidentally, did not approve of her extreme involvement in the folk group. She had no real boy friends and so had developed a safe, non-rejecting fantasy boy friend. The records and pictures had been reassuring to her and aided her fantasy that she was loved by someone. This removed her from the bind of competing with mother for father. When the pictures and reinforcements of her new-found separate identity were taken away, the old anxieties had returned and she felt alone, helpless, and depressed.

I suggested that she might continue to have the pictures, records and fantasy as long as she recognized it for what it was—a fantasy love. Helen appeared contented with this permission and left the appointment with no arrangements to return.

Stage III

Five months later, Helen called; she was overweight, anxious, not sleeping, dreaming a great deal, and worried about her fantasies. She came in and we arranged regular weekly appointments again.

She was most disturbed by what she felt was her father's intrusiveness. She thought he checked on her in her room too often, and noted that he looked into her purse whenever he saw it open. I supported these feelings, but reminded her that she had seemed quite close to her father when she was in the hospital and wondered what had changed her feelings. She allowed that he still was trying to be "nice," but that she "just could not talk to him anymore." She also did not talk to her mother, but denied that this was a problem.

Her dreams involved her father and her folk-group boy friend. In one dream she was entertaining her boy friend when her father came out and sent him away. In another she dreamed that her boy friend had been married. Her association to this was that she had not realized that "he was so old." I suggested that she appeared to see herself as a little girl, certainly too young to get married, yet really was a maturing young woman with feelings and needs to be loved as such. In one dream she had father sending boy friend away. She could thus be only his girl, the little girl of the second dream.

Helen thought back to her refusal to eat and noted her anger. She stated "Last time I was angry, I wouldn't eat, this time I shut myself away in my room." This incident and the interest in the folk group both served to avoid feeling completely dominated by her parents. She seemed also to be identifying with me. After being out of therapy for a time she had immediately noted that I now wore a wedding ring and had a new name. She appeared to be pleased, as though it were something happy that she shared.

She began to bring in material to share about a fellow whom she knew at school. Her fantasy life gradually shifted from her folk group friend to this new, "real," fellow. She noted his class shifts at school very carefully, his girl friends or lack of them, and was delighted whenever he looked at her or spoke to her.

On the other hand, when he ignored her she felt hurt and crestfallen, as though she had been rejected. She appeared to be working out her ambivalence about close relationships. She longed to have someone love and care for her, and yet was fearful of the consequences of separation.

As she presented material I again pointed out the real versus the fantasy nature of her thoughts about this boy. For instance, how could he really reject her if he did not even know her? She was able to give instances that illustrated her need *not* to get close to him. She would avoid open seats next to him in class. Another time she was to meet him after class but arranged to avoid him.

Helen was puzzled and disturbed about this aspect of her behavior. She further noted that it would be impossible for her to have a friendship with this boy because her time outside of classes was exclusively taken up by the girl friend who shared the folk group fantasy life. She described this relationship as nearly symbiotic, one in which they spent all their time planning to return to California, have an apartment together and pursue their fantasies about the folk group "boy friends." Even shopping trips were spent buying small furnishings for "their" apartment.

Helen soon felt a need to choose between spending her total time with this girl friend and finding new friends. She spent a great deal of time discussing fears about this girl's anger and jealousy and used me to support her separation. I compared this current dominant-submissive relationship to the one that I thought might have occurred between her and her mother. Just as mother had taken care of her and yet ignored her independent needs, this girl friend also took her to school, met her between classes, called her at home, but restricted her wish for new interests.

Several events aided Helen's separation—her classes shifted so that her free time changed and she indeed was free to find new girl friends in school clubs which she joined. She was chosen by one of her teachers to go on a summer guided tour with another group of classmates. This cinched it. She now could completely give up the idea of going to California, and was able to break with her girl friend.

She was coming to grips with feelings of being worthless and unwanted. She had become successful and popular in this, her last year of high school, and yet felt disappointment and failure. Her past illness was also a worry. She had wanted to be "pretty and famous" for her parents and family, but instead had embarrassed them by refusing to eat, not planning to go on in school, and chasing after a fantasy boy friend.

Helen sorted out plans for the future and decided upon a junior college in another city after her summer tour was over. She chose to be near an aunt whom she felt also had rebelled against the family and would understand her. We worked toward termination again. Not the least of her separations will be from nearly five years of therapy. She regards herself now as somewhat immature—especially in the realm of boys and dating—but feels confident and competent in her need to grow up and find her own role in life.

DISCUSSION

When Helen came to the psychiatric ward, well-meaning mentors insisted that she must be: schizophrenic, have oral impregnation fears, willfully disobedient, and that I should watch out for forced vomiting, food hiding, and other behaviors. I chose instead to keep staff anxiety and anger low while trying to understand first hand what caused the refusal to eat. Because she was *not* schizophrenic or severely neurotic she felt her own anxiety and wished for a healthy resolution of the problems besetting her. She could give up rejecting food and find other ways of expressing a wish for independence.

References

Bruch, H. (1965). "The psychiatric differential diagnosis of Anorexia Nervosa," *Anorexia Nervosa-Symposium in Gottigen*, G.T. Verfla (Ed.), Stuttgart, 70.

Related Reading

Bachrach, A.J., Erwin, W.J., and Mohr, J.P. (1965). "The control of eating behavior in an anorexic by operant conditioning techniques," in L.P. Ullman and L. Krasner (Eds.), *Case Studies in Behavior Modification,* New York: Holt, Rinehart and Winston.

Berkman, J.M. (1943). "Some clinical observations in cases of Anorexia Nervosa," *Proceedings of the Staff Meeting of Mayo clinic, 18,* 81.

Berlin, I.N., Boatman, M.J., Sheimo, S.L., and Szurek, S.A. (1951). "Adolescent alternation of anorexia and obesity," *American Journal of Orthopsychiatry, 21,* 387–419.

Binswanger, L. (1958). "The case of Ellen Terry," in R. May, E. Angel, and H. Ellenberger (Eds.), *Existence,* New York: Basic Books, ch. IX.

Blinder, B.J., Freeman, D.M.A., and Stunkard, A.J. (1970). "Behavior therapy of anorexia nervosa: effectiveness of activity as a reinforcer of weight," *American Journal of Psychiatry, 126,* 1093–1098.

Bliss, E.L., and Branch, C.H.H. (1960). *Anorexia Nervosa: Its History, Psychology and Biology,* New York: Hoever.

Dally, P. (1969). *Anorexia Nervosa,* London: William Heinemann Medical Books.

Forchheimer, F. (1951). "Anorexia nervosa in children," *Archives of Paediatrics, 68,* 35–45.

Lang, P.J. (1965). "Behavior therapy with a case of nervous anorexia," in L.P. Ullman and L. Krasner (Eds.), *Case Studies in Behavior Modification,* New York: Holt, Rinehart and Winston.

Lesser, L.I., Ashenden, B.J., Debuskey, M. and Eisenberg, L. (1960). "Anorexia nervosa in children," *American Journal of Orthopsychiatry, 30,* 572–580.

Meyer, J.E., and Feldmann, H. (1965). in G.T. Verfla (Ed.), *Anorexia Nervosa —Symposium in Gottigen,* Stuttgart.

Palmer, J.O., Meush, I.N., and Matarazzo, J.D. (1952). "Anorexia Nervosa," *Journal of Clinical Psychology, 8,* 168–173.

Rahman, L., Richardson, H.B., and Ripley, H.S. (1939). "Anorexia nervosa with psychiatric observations," *Psychosomatic Medicine, 1,* 335–365.

Rose, J.A. (1943). "Eating inhibitions in children in relation to anorexia nervosa," *Psychosomatic Medicine, 5,* 117–124.

Stunkard, A.J. (1957). "The 'dieting depression'," *American Journal of Medicine, 23,* 77–86.

Thoma, H. (1967). *Anorexia Nervosa,* New York: International Universities Press.

Winnicott, D.W. (1958). "Appetite and emotional disorder," in *Collected Papers,* London: Tavistock, ch. 3.

CHAPTER 8

Johnny - A Passive Aggressive, Selective Mute

HAROLD J. LOCKETT

WILLIAM C. MORSE

Editor's Introduction

The American conscience has been deeply pained by a relatively recent and intense awareness of the magnitude and permanence of disadvantages in our culture. These disadvantages come with no single condition but in many forms and often with a conglomerate of cultural or racial isolation, urban monotony, ghetto living, family instability, economic hardship, and inadequate education. A special form of concern comes with the convergence of blackness and poverty. This is where we find Johnny.

The case report suggests three important observations: a) the individual problem may be imbedded in social class or racial differences but it is nevertheless unique, a special set of reciprocal structures in which the individual responds to environment and experience, b) change may call for integrated, enduring and powerful intervention, and c) successful intervention may depend on a variety of treatments.

The program at Hawthorne has many of the characteristics advocated in other writings by Morse (1966, 1967). Briefly put, the child moves into a microcommunity designed for a special purpose. Education begins at once without waiting to achieve resolution of personality dynamics. Since the child's energy is absorbed in archaic preoccupations and because there are academic deficits the teacher is faced with special challenges. Success depends on: 1)*small classes,* 2) *placement* with a teacher who is sensitive but in charge, 3) *attention to motivation,* adapting to both levels of performance and case anxieties, and 4) *remediation* directed toward explicit shortcomings. In this chapter, Lockett and Morse describe an intimate joining of therapy with this education.

Comfortable union of therapy and academic teaching is not always the rule. Another expert, Nicholas Hobbs (1966), contends that an overcommitment to the psychiatric or sickness view has too often delayed getting at the problem. He and many others have believed that institutionalization too often results in children locked up and guarded to wait a "precious hour" which proves much too little. In effect, treatment for Johnny may lie roughly between two popular but quite different forms of treatment. One puts therapy, ordinarily analytic therapy, at the center of strategies (Klein, 1963; Bettelheim, 1967; Wolff, 1969). The other, often called a learning view, makes the assumption that maladjustments are learned in response to environment and may be unlearned in the same fashion (Hobbs, 1966; Hewett, 1967; Weinstein, 1969; Kravetz and Forness, 1971). The treatment is operant, contingency management, or an engineered classroom. This issue is discussed in chapter 1. The reader has an opportunity in Johnny's case to examine methodology at an applied level.

The cases of Johnny and Ken (chapter 4) deal with

children who are both economically disadvantaged and racially different. They show that there isn't one type "disadvantaged." There are divergences among such children, and these boys are but two of many. The reader might compare them with "Frankie," a case in Sears and Sherman, *In Pursuit of Self Esteem* (1964). It is in the school that most children first get feedback over failure, and it follows that institutionalized children are marked by academic as well as behavioral problems. In these problems and in institutions numbers of boys are significantly high (Bloch and Behrens, 1959). The case of Johnny raises many questions over the importance of environment, the adequacy of diagnoses and the effectiveness of treatment.

THE FIRST INTERVIEW

It took fully 10 minutes for him to come from the living area to the office, a distance usually covered in two minutes. His movements were extremely slow and deliberate. His eyes were half closed and his gaze downward. Facial expression was blank. This 13-year-old, well developed, well nourished, black youngster gave the impression of motion on a slowed film. As he approached he gave no response to verbal greeting except a sly smile and a fleeting glance. Even his handshake was flaccid. While he responded to requests requiring minimum physical involvement (for instance, the handshake, sitting down, etc.), not a word or vocal sound was heard. Here was a youngster not only selectively mute but also selectively kinetic.

There followed a conversation in which the boy demonstrated his awareness of surroundings, his comprehension of what was taking place, and his ability to respond, albeit in a nonverbal fashion. His eye movements and small changes in facial expression were indicators of desire as well as reluctance to respond. In later interviews the same week, questions requiring only a "yes" or "no" were answered with an appropriate nod of the head. While his most prevalent spontaneous response was a smile, his eyes were most expressive; they pleaded, questioned, showed anger, stubborness, disgust, warmth, ambivalence and were used manipulatively. Johnny had developed a system of almost complete nonverbal interaction to express his feelings and meet his environment. He had effectively sabotaged educational offerings. He was becoming more verbally withdrawn and his ability to learn or to utilize basic academic skills was rapidly moving toward a crucial state of atrophy from disuse.

In those first few encounters the problem became more clearly focused and our task more specifically delineated. The slide toward withdrawal had to be stopped and the embers of intellectual interest in the environment rekindled. Some way had to be found to energize his apparent intellectual ability. A comprehensive treatment program needed to be established immediately and pursued with vigor. Such a problem could be developed only in a multidisciplined facility. Johnny was assigned to a therapist who would see him for individual psychotherapy as well as coordinate his overall program. He was placed in a full remedial academic program, assigned to the language clinic for intensive study, and quartered in a structured living area where the impact of the milieu could be more clearly focused on his individual needs.

BACKGROUND

As the background unfolded it became apparent that Johnny's problems were more profound than recognized initially. Not only were his symptoms dramatic and chronic but several other agencies, including public schools, had been unsuccessful in intervention attempts. Indeed, the utter frustration of these services is typified when we note that Johnny came to Hawthorne Center from the detention home where he had been remanded as a temporary ward of the court some eight months earlier because of his lack of attendance at school. The neglect petition had been filed on his behalf by the local Board of Education.

Johnny's family consists of 16 individuals, 14 children ages 1 to 22 years, and the parents. The father, now in his mid-forties, was born and raised in a large Michigan city and attended public school only until the seventh grade. He is sensitive about this educational deficit. This is his second marriage. The court worker noted excessive sensitivity about his status as the head of the family and resentment of attempts to deal with the family through anyone but himself. He is described as a rather rigid, strict man who infrequently uses physical punishment but does verbally abuse the children when he is angry. He is a steady worker and has met the family's financial needs. In the past he was not steadily employed and was well known to welfare agencies. He is said to have very few, if any, close friends. He discourages visits to the home by outsiders, including the children's friends.

The mother, in her forties, was born in a large city in southern Ohio. She is a high school graduate. In 23 years of marriage there have been no known separations. The mother is described as "overwhelmed" by her many children and responsibilities, but manages the roles of mother and wife with a degree of success. She is not considered overly warm, but tends to be less rigid and strict with the children than her husband. She engages in more verbal interaction with the family than does the father. At the time of the initial evaluation, all 13 children were living at home. Since then the fourteenth child was born and the oldest girl, illegitimately pregnant, went to live with relatives. One other sister had an illegitimate pregnancy. The oldest boy enlisted in the army and currently is serving as a special corpsman. While none of the children has been a behavioral problem at school, there is a history of reluctance to talk to people outside the family group. The casework supervisor from the court interpreted the behavior of the children as "deviant behavior to symbolize their rebellion against some of the strict parental control allegedly exercised by the father." He saw Johnny's behavior as a "continuous rebellion against adult domination."

It is interesting to note the overall normal human reactions of these parents: pride, sensitivity, concern for the children, and reactions to overwhelming odds. It is not a family distinguished by extreme pathological interactions, but evident are many stresses common in low socioeconomic families. It is clear that individual strengths also presented obstacles to the usual mental health processes.

Johnny is the sixth child. The pregnancy was full term, uneventful, and the birth normal. The birthweight was within normal range. There was no indication of the biological atypicality often reported in center city children or temperamental deviation as noted by Chess. He was bottle fed and weaned within one year. There were no reported problems in development in the first year nor any history of significant physical illness. He was described as an active infant. Motor development proceeded normally. He walked unaided at 1 year. He began using monosyllabic words about 1 year and phrases shortly before his second birthday. Toilet training for both bowel and bladder was completed by age 2 without significant difficulty.

The mother noted nothing unusual about his behavior until age 3 when he began to have temper tantrums and nocturnal enuresis. At that time he refused to take naps in the afternoon. In an already overloaded and marginal family system, the response to this was intense. This unmanageableness angered and frustrated the mother sufficiently so that she resorted to typing his hands to the bed rail in order to keep him in bed. As he grew older, his tantrums increased and he indulged in destructive behavior with toys and other objects. Corporal punishment was frequent. Passive aggressive behavior in the form of select mutism was first noted before kindergarten. It appeared to develop in direct relationship to the use of punishment. It might be noted that other siblings in the family were also periodically selectively mute, both in the home and in the community. Johnny's refusal to speak, however, was felt to be the most severe. The mother felt that, at an early age, his "stubborness" was designed to inflict punishment in a retaliatory fashion on family members.

Medical history is not well documented, but as far as is known Johnny has been in good health. There is no evidence of seizures, significant head injury, or severe illness.

EARLY EDUCATIONAL EXPERIENCE

Johnny started kindergarten at age 5. There he refused to talk at all. When his mother came to school he would not even talk with her. He was "promoted" to the first grade the following year, but later demoted to a "reading readiness" level. In the ghetto environment, unless the school acts as advocate for the child's welfare, his problems are likely to be ignored. In this instance the school officials were concerned with Johnny's problems but uncertain of what to do. He was referred to a hospital clinic for evaluation at age 8 and this started the series of diagnostic appraisals which are usually more available than is treatment. Primary mental retardation was ruled out. There were estimates of "severe mental deprivation" and "suspicion of severe psychopathology of psychotic intensity." His drawing of the human figure suggested "serious emotional regression and a distorted body image." The drawings were "primitive" and "suggest possibility of regressed behavior and infantile emotionality."

His mutism made the usual intelligence assessment impossible, and this was the basis for referral to a special education class for emotionally disturbed pupils. His reluctance to attend school and his withdrawn behavior in the classroom added to the pressure for this special provision. It is to be noted that no plan was made for total treatment, family intervention, or even how the educational symptoms could be a path to treatment. There is no indication that the teacher was given any help in how to begin working with the child even on a limited basis. The labeling did not provide cues as to how Johnny viewed his life. At any rate he would not talk or do any tasks. He hated to go to school and would leave whenever he could. To Johhny the special class seemed like punishment; it added stress and increased defensive reactions because there was no real breakthrough to his view of life.

He failed to respond in school but he was comfortable at home. No problem was reported in the neighborhood recreational program or summer camp. Then he was examined by the school psychiatrist who recommended exclusion from the special class and in-patient treatment.

Such a recommendation faced dual obstacles: the availability of the service and family strengths which produced resistance. At any rate the recommendation was not followed, and he remained home from the fall of 1967 to mid-fall of 1968. The school then filed a neglect charge to force action on his behalf and by order of the court he was remanded to the community youth home where he lived and attended school. Like most crisis services, there are limitations in the length and intensity of possible service but it is important to note what removal of the family meant. According to the school reports, Johnny adjusted to the small sized class situation and showed some academic and social progress. He read and spelled aloud when requested. He was not made a scapegoat by peers and was relatively responsive to unit leaders. The youngsters said he could talk when he wanted to and he did talk spontaneously with some of his classmates. After one month of residence he returned home but continued to attend the youth home school.

Further study at the child clinic of the home produced doubt about any "ongoing psychotic process." Again, recommendation for psychiatric hospitalization for total treatment was made. This was actually the third such recommendation to the family. In reviewing the history of the family's contact with various agencies, including the school, it became clear that they were not fully cooperative probably both because of misunderstandings and because they had a deep desire to manage their own. Where possible, the father would terminate the contacts with the agency. The court involvement seemed necessary if any continued program was to be undertaken. Finally, a referral was made by the court to Hawthorn Center in January, 1968. Johnny was seen for evaluation a month later and was admitted as an in-patient in June, 1969.

TREATMENT PLAN

The treatment plan on entry to the hospital aimed to restore spontaneous verbal communication, to promote satisfactory interpersonal relations, to assess and begin remediation of academic deficits, and to uncover and modify the factors influencing the development of emotional problems. The psychological assessment at the time of the initial evaluation included the *Wechsler Intelligence Scale for Children.* Because he was nonverbal, he completed only the performance subtests and received a score of 83. There was evidence of potential for higher functioning.

Shortly after entering the hospital he was scheduled for a full day of school, recreational activities, individual psychotherapy, and a structured program in the general living area which included an opportunity for spontaneous interaction with peers and staff. Later, alternate weekend home visits were included. A staff social worker maintaining a close involvement with the family articulated with the therapist and other staff members who were planning Johnny's treatment experience.

In the school area he was assigned to a language clinic therapist who made an assessment of his problems and devised a program of remediation. This was an addition to the regular school program which included the subjects for his expected grade adapted to his level of functioning. Classes were small (eight to 10), fostering interaction between peers and with the teacher. In the living area he was housed in a room with three other boys, a part of a larger unit containing approximately 25 boys ranging in age from 8 to 16. Patient-staff ratio was approximately five to one. Living area activities were both structured and unstructured with unit, campus and outside activities. This affords opportunity for one-to-one relationships with peers or with staff as well as small and large group interaction. A given child's total program in the living area is guided by the overall rules and regulations but more specifically by the plan of handling worked out by the therapist in consultation with those who are in direct contact with the child.

The approach of the school and language clinic is educational and direct. There is a persistent expectation that the pupil really wants to learn, and he is expected to do his best. Diagnostic testing defines the task level and content. Patience, pressure, and praise represent the teacher's stance. In an atmosphere of quiet reassurance and a benign but not permissive relationship, the fears of exposing inability and meeting failure are mitigated. But with the seriously educationally handicapped embodied in a life-style it is a see-saw progression-regression process, slow and fragile as the child learns to cope.

It was initially decided that Johnny be allowed to interact at whatever level he wished with peers and staff in all areas. This was designed to allow for the spontaneous development of behavior in response to a structured or controlled environment. Later, after observation and evaluation, specific handling procedures were devised to implement the program leading to the goals. These specific interactions and the proposed handling techniques were discussed in the psychotherapeutic interviews with Johnny. As a result of this approach his initial encounters in the living area with staff and children were nonverbal. He was seen as warm and communicative, but unresponsive to any attempts by staff or peers to engage in verbal communication. His peers began to accept his nonverbal approach and engaged him in games. Whenever his nonverbal approaches were ignored he became passive and motorically retarded. He became tearful when he was the inadvertent victim of aggressive action by other children, but no overt counteraggression was noted. He obeyed instructions concerning various routines, including going to school, but he was extremely slow in responding.

After his initial nonverbal adjustment, it was decided that verbal participation, at least at a minimum level, would be the next goal. With selectively mute children, both initial traumatic forcing and prolongation of mute behavior are to be avoided. Following adjustment to the new life, extended nonverbal interaction deters recovery and promotes withdrawal. Johnny did, indeed, want to be with other children, and at least physically in the area, if not in the activity. More than that, he enjoyed one-to-one attention, but in all instances he attempted to dominate the situation in a covertly passive, nonverbal fashion.

A stimulus-response technique was designed to promote verbal interaction. Broad guidelines were drawn with specific requirements for minimal verbal interaction. Attached to these were a series of isolative techniques to emphasize and reinforce the positive response and to reduce negative reaction. All involved staff members including his teachers were advised of the goals and the behavioral prescription. The therapist described and explained the design to Johnny in an attempt to secure his cooperation. Of course, Johnny tried to continue his silent control of the situation even in the face of minimal requests, but his efforts were unsuccessful. As a result his overt negativism increased. Johnny focused hostile feelings on the therapist. In spite of this, he was able to follow the prescribed pattern with relatively infrequent use of persuasion. Within the first few weeks of hospitalization his verbal and physical response to staff and children increased significantly. His participation in activities was increasingly spontaneous and gratifying.

The concomitant increase in overt hostility was discussed in therapy and began the "working-through" process. Extinction of negative acting out was accomplished through the use of partial isolative bed restrictions for varying lengths of time, according to his responsiveness. Expression of hostility was encouraged within the framework of the patient-therapist interaction rather than through the regressive acting out represented by selective mutism and psychomotor retardation. Within two months, physical and verbal activity was within the normal range. There were, however, periodic regressive episodes, usually related to hostile content coming to conscious level.

While Johnny never presented major behavioral problems, it became clear that he had definite opinions about what he should or should not have to do. He began to identify with some of the more aggressive peers, although he did not participate in their aggression. While he was basically compliant, he began vocalizing reluctance to accept the hospital program, "the routine." He wanted greater freedom and more participation in the development of his own program. He would become verbally negative with the staff and would often accuse them of not carrying out their duties or of ignoring some of his legitimate requests. However, he continued to adjust realistically in the living area. Most of his conflicts with the program, as well as his feeling about his "freedom" were discussed in therapy and were extended to include his dissatisfaction with his general environment prior to hospitalization. While he wanted to be at home, which he saw as affording greater freedom, he recognized that some aspects of the program, particularly the school, were not only helpful but crucial to his future.

His performance status at the end of June (1969) was assessed by the language clinic. He was now 12 years, 11 months.

Gates Oral	1.7
Gates Primary A	
vocabulary	1.2
comprehensive	1.2
arithmetic	2.7
spelling	1.5

At first he would respond verbally only to oral test items and not in conversation. His instructional level was primer. In August his classroom teacher reported, "He is doing well in the *Sullivan Series*—adds and subtracts and can spell some first grade words—excellent progress." Further, he responded with a few words to questions, was friendly, liked by peers, and seemed to enjoy school. As his mutism subsided, school progress increased. Within a very few months he was functioning at his highest level ever. He always completed an assignment although he was slow in initiating the process. His negativism was not a factor at this time and he seemed gratified with his progress and responded well to praise. However, the deficits were significant. His reading

was six years below grade expectation. Assessment revealed
no impairment of the ability to acquire basic skills, but
rather marked delay in acquisition of those skills with some
concomitant atrophy from disuse/lack of exposure. His conceptual ability more closely approximated grade level expectations and his speaking vocabulary was higher than his
reading vocabulary. As motivation improved, his relationships with his teachers, particularly his reading therapist,
became more actively positive.

His first school test in September on the *California
Achievement Test* shows a total grade score of 1.9:

reading	1.6
arithmetic	2.5
English-spelling	1.9
total:	1.9

By October his teacher reports his completion of mathematics book I but he has trouble with subtraction. He shows some
spontaneity and has begun to take part in class discussions.
He seems to comprehend a great deal from just listening.

Interestingly, he now talks a lot but in an immature tone
of voice, and will not keep quiet when he should. "He tries
to do whatever he feels like." If one assumes his mute resistance was to protect his existence, then his current psychological behavior seems to be the same with the symptom
reversed—not letting outside influences determine his
course of action and thereby diminish the power and self-
ness.

By November he is slow to get started but completes his
assignments: he is doing well in mathematics III, and reads
at a higher level but he needs help with words. His ability to
use the school environments has increased and his negativism is diminished as he works hard for approval.

In December his language clinic test retest scores are as
follows:

Gates Oral	2.4
Gates Primary	
vocabulary	2.2
comprehensive	1.6
arithmetic	3.0
spelling	1.5

At this time he has hit a slump, with less involvement and
more effort at getting out of work. His progress is slower. His
social behavior shows more reserve and less relationship
with his teacher.

Individual Psychotherapy

The ultimate goal in psychotherapy was to produce greater autonomy and more integrated functioning. In the initial interviews the therapist was very active and direct in describing inappropriate behavior, distortions in conceptions of environment, and misinterpretations of relationships. Expectations for change were described and discussed and reasons given for the methods used to reinforce them. No goal was suggested that was not clearly attainable within a reasonable length of time. He was encouraged to respond to the prescription for immediate change and to aid in establishment of short- and long-term goals.

Minimal verbal communication was the initial goal. He received constant feedback in the living and school areas as well as in the office sessions. Alternatives and consequences of his choice were clearly delineated. While much of the initial time was spent in working toward prescribed goals, there was an increasing segment of time for spontaneous, nondirected behavior. The patient-therapist relationship was used as an opportunity for developing corrective interpersonal experience. This was extended to include interactions with the staff in school and living areas.

We were able to assess several aspects of his personality, including the most frequently used defense mechanisms, and to explore the possible reasons for the selection of those mechanisms. It became clear that he was an intelligent youngster who had adequate capacity for relationships but used passive-aggressive techniques as a method of expressing hostility. His social and intellectual concepts were basically intact. As his involvement in the program developed, it became more feasible for him to express his feelings verbally since the response to his nonverbal approach did not result in his continued control of the environment. He explored the therapist-patient relationship in both negative and positive aspects. Further, he interacted more constructively with his environment, resulting in more efficient use of time and energy.

Improved communication pointed up his intellectual ability and basic curiosity as well as his need for more social contacts. He possessed a surprisingly wide range of information, evidencing a higher level of interest and absorption than his history seemed to indicate. He was able to examine his desires, interests, and frustrations in therapy sessions and make suggestions about his living problems. The relationship with the therapist served to stimulate new interests, dispel the pervasive feeling of hopelessness and need to withdraw, and the fear of inadequate control of hostility. Progress in therapy was slow and measured.

He initially placed his ambitions for future occupation no higher than his father's present level. His anticipated efforts were to be directed toward earning enough money to live comfortably. After considerable exploration of his feelings and of other possible life styles he began to place value in the possibility of achieving primary gratification from an occupation with secondary gains being financial. He expressed interest in, and surprising knowledge of areas of science and medicine. As his reading ability improved he spontaneously picked up medical periodicals in the office and asked knowledgeable questions about articles and pictures. His most intuitive areas of interest involved people. His assessments of peers and staff were insightful. His ability to evaluate the current problems in the society both on local and national levels gave an indication of his conceptual development as well as his sensitivity to the needs of people. He was very much aware of the meaning of being black in our society. The accompanying hostile feelings were present but surprisingly controlled.

He now tended to talk less of his past, particularly about his family. The ambivalence toward his parents, particularly his father, was clear in the content elicited. The therapeutic goal at this point was to help him achieve a balanced view of positive and negative factors and role models in his past and a realistic appraisal of assets, deficits, and potential for a reconstructed future. Acquisition of academic skills, particularly reading, became more important and received a greater allotment of energy or effort.

While he initially resented being dependent, he came to view it as a "necessary evil." Gradually he was able to see that there was a normal dependency which need not become overwhelming or create impotency. He later recognized the existence of mutual dependency which implies a reciprocal relationship between equals. He was able to "accept" some of the limitations imposed by his background and those existing in the hospital. It was under these circumstances that his posthospital program was defined. His continued need for intensive academic help precluded returning home and to public school. He recognized these needs and accepted the delay. Placement was made in an open group living facility where he could attend Hawthorn Center Day Care Program. This disposition was approximately one year after his initial admittance.

At the end of January, things were moving better: spontaneity was up, he was involved and paying attention. He knew his multiplication tables and some division. By March he was doing well in a second grade speller, fourth grade math, and working actively in social studies. He was happier in class relating to peers and the teacher. He participated and interacted even during free time. He showed a good sense of humor. Things were encouraging, but the teacher recognized the thin margin and the many "adjustments" provided in the special school and milieu, warning that he should not yet go to public school. Often, just when things are moving, we expect too much, not realizing how situationally responsive performance is.

By April he had learned to use cursive writing, and was being pushed to produce more work. The lack of use of phonetic skills was apparent. He had some playful peer conflicts, responded well to humor, and was being teased. His school test scores on the *California Achievement Test* were:

reading	2.0
arithmetic	3.2
English-spelling	2.0
total:	2.3

In seven months there was a gain of four months. This, incidentally, corresponds to our general finding. Children who are seriously educationally retarded (but without organic signs) have a much lower than average slope to their academic growth curve. Thus the longer they are helped, the more they gain but they continue to fall away from the norm expectancy.

In May his teacher noted he was doing well in the academic and social aspects of the classroom, but he needed constant drill because he forgot previously learned skills. He had some manual and artistic skills which might be capitalized on in special ways. His July language clinic test results were:

Gates Oral	2.9
Gates Primary A	
vocabulary	2.3

comprehensive	3.0
arithmetic	3.8
spelling	2.3

While these are hardly a "spurt" they do represent consistent improvement in all areas.

Throughout his stay, the language clinic has been working one-to-one cooperatively with his teacher on academics. For six months his language therapy was characterized by lethargic one word answers after "prodding." The second half of the year he began to communicate and show an interest in books and reading.

His language teacher stated that for a 13-year-old boy, he was severely retarded in reading. He had no word attack skills and a very limited sight vocabulary. The reading program began with a dual emphasis on phonetics and sight vocabulary. Progress was very slow the first six months. He found he could learn sight vocabulary and became involved. He learned most of the letter sounds, consonant blends, and many word parts. His therapist used *Phonics We Use,* and the Dolch, *My Puzzle Book* as well as games. Johnny himself chose Wagner's *The Mystery of Morgan Castle* to read. His attitude was good but continued assistance seemed essential. The program was word attack skills, sight vocabulary and reading for meaning in a very small group or tutorial situation.

In fall of the second year he made a reasonable adjustment from his woman teacher to a new room with a male teacher. He did most of his assignments as requested, but worked slowly and needed prodding. Two months later he was doing well on a one-to-one relationship but not independently. His investment was low, and he remained by himself at free time. In December the *California Achievement Test* results were:

reading	2.9
arithmetic	4.3
English-spelling	3.5
total:	3.7

In these eight months, he gained 1.4 years, significant progress. It is worth noting that he had not demonstrated his growth in class, he regressed to previous modes of adjustment in the new educational situation. By January, he was making progress but was guarded in giving his teacher any cues about his real capabilities. His peers were friendly but he was uninvolved.

In March, at age 14 years and 8 months, his language clinic scores were:

Gates Oral	4.0
Gates-MacGinity Primary C	
vocabulary	3.9
comprehensive	4.3
Gates Basic Reading	
comprehensive	4.2
arithmetic	5.0
spelling	2.3

He would have scored 5.0 on the oral portion except for carelessness. By May of the second year his final *California Achievement Test* results show slow but steady progress:

reading	3.9
arithmetic	4.5
language	3.8
total	4.1

He continues to make gains and is working diligently. His motivation is tenuous.

The WISC was repeated in 1970 at which time he completed both the performance and verbal parts of the test. He scored a verbal scale of 79 and performance scale of 97. Subtest scores on the verbal scale were predictive of average potential. There was significant improvement on "performance" subtests. All scores were up except Block Design. The psychologist felt that he had at least average ability with probable higher potential.

The ebb and flow of his educational experience is part of the whole therapeutic picture. Many youngsters, at his age, give up rather than persist when progress is so difficult. He has so far to go educationally, that no placement plans can be considered without the availability of special education. His behavior problems are arrested and in fact were never very difficult for skilled teachers, but without protection through adolescence, he stands to lose what has been gained.

INTERPRETATION

Unlike many ghetto children, Johnny finally did get help. He is a psychoneurotic youngster with both internalized and externalized features. These characteristics result from several factors, including partial emotional neglect, his position in a highly competitive family situation, socioeconomic factors affecting the family, and the socioeducational climate of his community. He is a middle child in a very large sibship. His emotional needs were only partially met by a mother overwhelmed by the needs of many children. His negativism became apparent early in his life when the mother found it necessary to deter or alter his level of spontaneity. She attempted to routinize his activity to fit into family life. His initial response was increased temper outbursts but this later gave way to a passive negativism which he apparently found successful in demonstrating hostility and frustration.

There had been previous episodes of selective mutism occuring in the family and these had gained attention otherwise not available. In this relatively rigid setting Johnny's only defense against his growing hostility was to act out passively and speak cautiously, if at all. These characteristics reduced his educational opportunity. He avoided school whenever possible, and he behaved in a negative fashion when he did attend. He refused to participate in exercises designed to give evidence of educational growth. As his frustrations with the school setting grew, so did the tenacity of his negativism. He was almost willfully defiant, and used that defiance to control his environment and his interpersonal relations. At the time of the initial evaluation he presented the stereotypical picture of a passive-negative, motorically retarded, but somewhat pleasant appearing, controlling youngster.

The modes available for identification, principally his parents and neighborhood adults, used many similar adjustments to maneuver or manipulate their environment. Johnny had some insight into racial relations and this increased his defensive patterns, diverting psychic energy which could have been used for more constructive activity. While he understood the need for some conformity, the need to resist was even greater because of his fear of being completely controlled or rejected. The prototypical example was that of his father who resisted conforming but at great emotional cost and without much success. The father's attempt to express masculinity by playing the role of the strong, autonomous father led to rigidity and partial neglect of his children. The father, and Johnny following him, developed low self-esteem based on a combination of personal, racial, class and economic factors. Both had difficulty discriminating the boundaries of self-imposed limits and those imposed by society. In Johnny, the feeling of frustration and the use of withdrawal as controlling behavior contributed to educational retardation. He was reactive to both social and family forces, which, in turn were related one to the other. In spite of this, his character is less distorted than might be expected. He is less neurotic than involved in an attempt to control noxious or potentially noxious conditions. Energy, which would have been consumed in the effort to handle internalized conflicts, thus was relatively free for use in assessment of his social and academic environment. Much of this energy, however, was used to compete with other family members for the limited fund of attention and to avoid retaliation. His innate abilities suffered from disuse in these formative years.

Identification was a pivotal issue in therapy. The role models available to Johnny in his early years were at best ambivalently perceived, thus precluding the development of a clear, consistent positive self-image. The inferior status assigned to blacks in our society influenced his self-appraisal, and the models immediately available tended to reinforce this image.

The involvement with a black therapist, as well as other black staff who possessed status and power in a heterogeneous multi-racial setting, afforded an opportunity for reassessment of innate abilities and correction of some negative self-appraisal. Individual therapy intensified the relationship, taking full advantage of such an interactional opportunity. The course of therapy clearly shows a gradual shifting of identification, a lessening of frustration, an increasing ability to evaluate self and a higher self-esteem.

There is clear evidence of a significant improvement in Johnny's chances for greater fulfillment of his potential in all areas. However, the influence of his early circumstances on the personality remains profound and will continue to be a factor in the future. Indeed, many of those experiences in addition to the basic intactness of the early ego were the necessary substrata on which therapy could build and alter negatively developing trends. The inaccessibility of this boy to the regular school system or the inability of the system to gain access to him was almost educationally fatal. The system must be held accountable for the depths of his unfortunate responses to school. While the general prognosis is favorable, the educational prognosis appears limited because much support is needed to counter these inadequate early experiences.

Efforts to stimulate emotional and academic growth were successful after removal of some of the more superficially oppressive aspects of his environment and the rigidity of life style. He was encouraged to use his energies more efficiently and more productively. Once he was able to view himself and his potential in more realistic light, his spontaneity returned and his motivation remarkably improved. Johnny's prognosis for continued growth is excellent. The limitations on that growth will be more specifically determined by his efforts and by the losses in his formative school years.

References

Bettelheim, B. (1967). *The Empty Fortress: Infantile Autism and the Birth of the Self,* New York: The Free Press.

Bloch, D.A. (1959) and Behrens, M.L., *A Study of Children Referred for Residential Treatment in New York State,* Albany, N.Y. State Interdepartmental Health Resource Board.

Hewett, F.M. (1967). "Educational engineering with emotionally disturbed children," *Exceptional Children, 33,* 459–467.

Hobbs, N. (1966). "Helping disturbed children: Psychological and ecological strategies," *American Psychologist, 21,* 1105–1115.

Klein, M. (1963). *The Psychoanalysis of Children,* London: Hogarth Press.

Kravetz, R.J. and Forness, S.R. (1971). "The special classroom as a desensitization setting," *Exceptional Children, 37,* 389–391.

Morse, W.C. (1967). "The education of socially maladjusted and emotionally disturbed children," in W.M. Cruickshank and G.O. Johnson (Eds.) *Education of Exceptional Children and Youth,* 2nd ed., Englewood Cliffs, N.J.: Prentice Hall, 598–608.

Morse, W.C. (1966). "Preparing to teach the disturbed adolescent," *The High School Journal, 69,* 259–265.

Sears, P.S. and Sherman, V.S. (1964). *In Pursuit of Self Esteem: Case Studies of Eight Elementary School Children,* Belmont, California: Wadsworth, 114–132.

Weinstein, L. (1969). "Project Re-ed Schools for emotionally disturbed children: Effectiveness as viewed by referring agencies, parents and teachers," *Exceptional Children, 35,* 703–711.

Wolff, S. (1969). *Children Under Stress,* London: Penguin, 194–215.

Related Reading

Cohen, H. (1963). "The academic-activity program at Hawthorne: A specially designed educational program for the troubled adolescent," *Exceptional Children, 30,* 74–79.

Grossman, H. (1968). *Teaching the Emotionally Disturbed: A Casebook,* New York: Harper and Row.

Hewett, F.M. (1968). *The Emotionally Disturbed Child in the Classroom. A Developmental Strategy for Educating Children with Maladaptive Behavior,* Boston: Allyn and Bacon.

Johnson, J.L. and Rubin, E.Z. (1964). "A school follow-up of children from a psychiatric hospital," *Exceptional Children, 31,* 19–24.

Miller, N. (1969). "Language therapy with an autistic non-verbal boy," *Exceptional Children, 35,* 555–557.

Hobbs, N. (1966). "Helping disturbed children: Psychological and ecological strategies," *American Psychologist, 21,* 1105–1115.

Kravetz, R.J. and Forness, S.R. (1971 "The special classroom as a desensitization setting," *Exceptional Children, 37,* 389–391.

Morse, W.C. (1966). "Preparing to teach the disturbed adolescent," *The High School Journal, 69,* 259–265.

Morse, W.C. (1967). "The education of socially maladjusted and emotionally disturbed children," in W.M. Cruickshank and G.O. Johnson (Eds.) *Education of Exceptional Children and Youth,* 2nd ed., Englewood Cliffs, N.J.: Prentice Hall, 598–608.

Vacc, N.A. (1968). "Study of emotionally disturbed children in regular and special classes," *Exceptional Children, 35,* 197–204.

Yule, W. and Rutter, M. (1968). "Educational aspects of childhood maladjustment: Some epidemiological findings," *British Journal of Educational Psychology, 38,* 7–9.

Underpriviledged

Ausubel, D.P. (1964). "How reversible are the cognitive and motivational effects of cultural deprivation? Implications for teaching culturally deprived children," *Urban Education, 1,* 16–38.

Bloom, B.S., Davis, A. and Hess, R.D. (1965). *Compensatory Education for Cultural Deprivation,* New York: Holt, Rinehart and Winston.

Clark, K. (1965). *Dark Ghetto,* New York: Harper and Row.

Coleman, J.S.; Campbell, E.Q.; Hobson, C.J.; McPartland, J.; Mood, A.M.; Weinfield, F.D.; York, R.L.; (1966). *Equality of Educational Opportunity,* Washington, D.C.: U.S. Department of Health, Education and Welfare, U.S. Printing Office.

Fantini, M.D. and Weinstein, G. (1968). *The Disadvantaged: Challenge in Education,* New York: Harper and Row.

Jensen, A.R. (1968). "Social class, race and genetics: Implications for education," *American Education Research Journal, 5,* 18–23.

Passow, A.H., Goldberg, M. and Tannenbaum, A.J. (1967). *Education of the Disadvantaged,* New York: Holt, Rinehart and Winston.

CHAPTER 9

Tina and Barry - Learning Problems and Family Counseling

ROBERT T. ELLIOTT

Editor's Introduction

In this chapter, Dr. Elliott reviews two cases which came to his attention through school problems and were treated in an active, family counseling model. The focus is on contemporary confusions and task performance more than psychogenic factors. The professional is active or direct: (even directive), and the family is involved not simply as background, but as fundamental in the problem and in the therapy.

The intentional involvement of family in psychotherapy is nothing new but the purpose and management of this involvement has changed. A strong relation between family life and child behavior is universally observed. "Crazy" behavior often begins to make sense when the family is known, for each family has unique rules, alliances, and fears. The child's role in that family manifests both individual and multiperson controls.

Prior to 1955, parents or siblings usually were

brought into parallel therapy or consultative sessions either for their own benefits or to enhance the treatment of the designated patient by a) defusing unconscious conflicts, b) avoiding clashes between parental and therapist expectations, c) reducing parental anxiety and urgency, d) helping parents maintain conditions which enhance progress, e) solving a family problem damaging to the patient, and f) economizing therapy by the spread of effect to other children and to many aspects of the client's life. Family members, most often the mother, were brought in as helpers (Furman, 1950). This is quite different from the current emphasis on communication theory employed to deal with sickness in relationships themselves.

Therapists in the earlier period were aware of complex interactions such as the intense symbiosis between mother and schizophrenic child, with the father in some fashion a participant in maintaining the pathology (Hill, 1955). They found that treatment collapsed from strain in the family or that progress halted after insight was achieved because insight alone could not support behavioral change in repressive or pathologic families. The illness analogy lent some support to the individual treatment rationale; models that depended on intrapsychic data made it difficult to work in teams and almost impossible to place parents in central roles and beyond that psychological constructs and measurements in individual terms did not facilitate family treatment.

Nevertheless group and family treatment first were undertaken out of the analytic tradition and much of the work continues to show that influence (Friedman, Boszormenyi-Nagy, Jungreis, Lincoln, Mitchell, Sonne, Speek and Spivak, 1965; Satir, 1967; Jackson, 1968). Guiding the work with schizophrenics was a growing conviction that intrapsychic and transactional worlds not only had to be related or articulated but also fully integrated.

Some of the more popular transitional practices were

developed by the new-Adlerians who insisted the task was educational and not medical and therefore both relatively public and within the competence of sensible people with a little guidance (Dreikurs, 1968). The child must learn strategies for self-assertion and these are social tasks. Learning from either life or therapy results in social interest, courage, and common sense. If learning is to take place there must be a demand for coping or compensation for these inferiorities may turn the child to the "useless side" and he becomes self-safeguarding or insatiable with putting others in his service. The neurotic or special forms of compensation have been studied in relation to birth order, attention-getting mechanisms, and distance-seeking behaviors. The resulting paradigms are simple and categorical and in these qualities the explanations are like models for the current "modes of relating" and "transactional process." In both cases, the treatment methodology includes parent training, particularly training in the use of differential encouragements.

Another program of parent training is called "filial therapy" (Guerney, 1964). The overtones are analytic and Rogerian, the purpose is to help the parent learn to use play therapy, reflection, clarification of feelings, and other procedures to work with a child in the direction of freer communication, reduced repression, and released feeling.

The parent training model now is widely advocated sometimes in a specific family and often in a general program (Patterson, Ray and Shaw, 1968; Walder, Kohen, Breiter, Daston, Hirsch and Leibowitz, 1969; Mathis, 1971; Gordon, 1970). The parents participate in study groups or programmed instruction. They are trained to observe, and the exemplar may demonstrate sample interventions or, through role playing, the parent finds and tests previously untried responses. Some trainers give major attention to development of family councils, analysis of communication modes, and teaching in a participatory or consulting style. Others attend to talk analysis and sequencing with definitive objectives and criteria of performance for each subtask on the route to a target behavior. They favor teaching in a precision or operant style. In any case, the major education or therapy ordinarily occurs in the absence of the professional.

Parent trainers concentrate on socialization and accomplishment with pscyhic integrity at most an associated benefit. Active goals probably are understood and popular with parents. The methods, too, are for the most part simple, step-at-a-time, and within parental understanding and capacity. We cannot here review the several programs but most would endorse the Adlerian principles suggested by Rudolph Dreikurs (1964) for example: maintain routine, sidestep the struggle for power, stimulate independence, stay out of fights, listen, watch your voice, respect the child, encourage the child, etc.

The Center for Psychological and Educational Services is more aptly designated as a family counseling than parent training agency. The reports on Tina and Barry show that the counseling session is seen as important experience in itself and perhaps also as parental development. Tina is an example of a type often discussed. A mother with uncertain or low self-assurance expects too much and simultaneously fears disappointment. In consequence she gives incongruent messages to her daughter (Satir, 1967). Both children demonstrate that one person in a family may project into another and try to solve problems there. It follows that the referral to a "presenting patient" often brings in an interlocking family system and improvement in that patient may cause decline in another family member, since all are part of a homeostatic multiperson structure.

A POINT OF VIEW

Management of learning and behavior disorders has changed greatly in 20 years. In the early fifties emphasis was on the child's emotional life and his intrapsychic conflicts. The treatment of choice was psychotherapy for the child and related counseling for the parents. This approach seemed to help some children, but not others. In the early sixties we discovered the "neurology of learning" and large numbers of children were diagnosed as having minimal cerebral disfunction and/or perceptual learning problems. The treatment methods for this group centered about motor and perceptual retraining. This approach seemed to help some children, but not all. In the late sixties articles appeared in professional journals pointing out that labeling children often caused the labeler and others to view the child in a stereotyped manner (Rosenthal, 1968). Labeling a child might cause the therapist to use an inappropriate method and compound the problem. The argument was that labeling and categorizing might be appropriate when a physician made a diagnosis of measles, but the gross labels of mental retardation, emotional disturbance, and minimal cerebral dysfunction were too broad to effectively communicate a description of the child that had meaning for treatment purposes. This awareness of misfunctioning labels in educational circles was basic to a new approach in clinics and classrooms.

The emphasis is on task analysis and principles of teaching, a focus on what the child is doing now, what the task is before him, and what the steps are to learn to perform this task. This approach stays away from labels or causation but makes use of what has been learned about motivation, learning, and teaching technology (Bateman, 1971). At the same time as teachers and psychologists were questioning previous methods of teaching children with learning disorders, a similar revolution was going on in psychiatric clinics and hospitals concerning the methods of psychotherapy (Burton, 1969; Perls, 1969). There were experiments with new methods such as encounter groups, sensitivity training, gestalt therapy, and family therapy.

The staff at the Center for Psychological and Educational Services has been influenced by these two trends, task analysis in teaching and the use of a health and growth model in psychotherapy. We came together as people from different disciplines to provide multiple services to children and adults with learning and behavioral disorders. The children who come to us exhibit a wide range of behaviors and problems. Primarily they are school failures. Many of these children also are in extreme conflict within their own families. Rare indeed is the child who is not also part of a family in crisis. This is not to agree with the position that parents *cause* the child's problems, but rather to point out that parents care about their children and are part of their growth and development, both positive and negative, and that problems rarely occur in isolation.

In our early attempts to work with these children and their learning problems we made primary use of task analysis in working with the child's learning problem, operant conditioning techniques to eliminate behaviors that interfere with learning, and psychotherapy and parent counseling to help the child resolve his inter- and intrapersonal conflicts. As we progressed, we found that even though we could help a child improve his learning, we were not always successful in helping him resolve his personal conflicts with parents, peers, and teachers so that he could make use of his new skills and become an effective learner.

As we assessed ourselves and our methods it became clear that we needed a reevaluation and conceptualization of our treatment procedures. It was at this time that we turned to family therapy. We retained all of our prior techniques including psychotherapy, but began looking at children and families differently. We perceive ourselves as treating families, not children in isolation, nor part of the child, such as his "learning disability" or his emotional problems.

Family treatment is a point of view and not a technique. Our procedures vary from seeing the child in educational therapy and the parents once a month for consultation, to seeing the child once a week in educational therapy and the entire family in a conjoint session once a week. We use different combinations and time sequences but our overriding point of view is that the child is part of an interactional system. The nature of this interaction must be considered and treated if the child is to be helped with his learning problems and to make an effective adjustment in school and society.

It may be useful to review some concepts concerning family interaction that we have found helpful in our work. First is the concept of family homeostasis. This refers to the observation that the family forms a dynamic, steady-state system. Each member is interdependent and interactional. As the family grows in time and space, the unit shifts to accommodate new growth but tends to keep the status quo.

The family will change, but resist change at the same time.

Second is the concept of the presenting patient. Parents come to our Center and say in effect, "Here, Johnny has a problem. Fix him up." The child may well have a problem. However, in most cases Johnny and how he responds to his problem also are symptomatic of a disorder in the family. In addition to the child's reading problem, mother and father may not be getting along, sister is acting out sexually or brother may be near psychotic. The presenting patient often is the disordered family's way of asking for help for another member or family dysfunction.

Third is the double bind. Communication is the chief means of human interaction and influence, but a single, simple message never occurs. Communication always and necessarily involves a simultaneous multiplicity of messages at different levels. These can be conveyed via various channels such as words, tone, and facial expressions or by the variety of meanings and references of any verbal message in relation to its possible context. No two messages at different levels of communication can be just the same. However, they may be similar or different; congruent or incongruent. The double bind refers to a pattern of pairs or sets of messages at different levels which are closely related, but sharply incongruent. These occur together with other messages which by concealment, denial, or other means seriously hinder the recipient from clearly noticing the incongruence and handling it effectively, as by commenting on it. A mother might be saying, "I want to do everything for my child that is possible," but the second part of that message is, "If you ask me for anything I will deny it." The father may say, "I want my son to be outgoing and aggressive; however, if you try it with me I will pin your ears back." The double bind also reflects in the "presenting patient concept" and the "family homeostasis" idea. The family may be hurting and will bring the patient for help, but in effect will say, "We want help but don't change the family," thereby blocking any appropriate assistance for the child.

TINA

Tina was brought to the Center as a sixth grader at 12 years, 11 months of age. Her mother was concerned about Tina's school progress. Tina was failing in almost all of her subjects, with major disabilities in reading and math. The mother was concerned that even though these problems had been with Tina all through her school career, she now was demonstrating additional emotional problems: she was becoming resentful, had developed a poor self-concept, and no longer was trying to achieve in school.

School History

Tina's school history indicates that her problems were noted in kindergarten where she showed mild, gross and fine motor coordination problems. Tina was retained in first grade due to lack of progress. During the second grade her school adjustment problems became more prominent. Often she would come home crying and it became obvious that she was far behind the other children. The third, fourth, and fifth grades brought repetitive reports. The mother had made various attempts to work with the school. Tina had been tested by school psychologists; consultation had been given to teachers; however, Tina was not eligible for any special program. The parents' military connections had involved many moves from one school to another preventing continuity in Tina's educational program.

Developmental History

Tina's developmental history indicates that she achieved the major development milestones within a normal period. However, she was a colicky baby and the mother indicated that Tina was subject to projectile vomiting. The mother also noted that in Tina's first year, she was a "rocker" and slept at only two or three hours at a time. She tended to be hyperactive in these early years and displayed some gross motor and fine motor coordination problems. Tina is left handed. She rode a bicycle at 8 years of age and her mother feels that she was always a little clumsy.

Family

Tina's family consists of a sister, Cher, age 10, and another sister, Sonny, age 9. The father, a pilot in the Air Force, is gone a great deal. The mother has been responsible for most of the child rearing as is common in military families where the husband often is on remote duty. In our first contacts, the mother stated that things were fine in the family, there were no marital difficulties, and no problems with the other children. It was obvious that Tina was the "presenting patient."

Test Results

As part of the intake process, Tina was given both psychological and educational tests. On the *Wechsler Intelligence Scale for Children* she received a verbal scale IQ of 91, a performance scale IQ of 96, and full scale IQ of 93. She showed a wide inter- and intra-test variability, gave up easily, and found it difficult to express herself. It was the examiner's opinion that these were minimal measurements and that Tina's potential was higher than the computed IQ scores.

On the *Bender Visual Motor Gestalt Test,* Tina displayed some mild fine motor coordination problems. Primarily the execution of designs suggested immaturity and emotional construction rather than any overt organicity. On the *Durrell Analysis of Reading Difficulty* she scored third grade, five months. Her reading performance was characterized by hesitations, omissions, and insertions. On the *Wide Range Achievement Test,* Tina scored at fourth grade, five months in arithmetic. An analysis of these test scores indicated a number of learning problems. Tina was low in specific and factual information. She had difficulty in applying information and in generalizing from one situation to another. In arithmetic she needed to develop attention to the details and processes in simple division, fractions, borrowing, two place multiplication, and decimals. She showed an extreme deficit in word knowledge and a deficit in immediate and long-term memory. In general, Tina's cognitive functioning was characterized by difficulty in assimilating new information into prior learning. Consequently she had difficulty in applying learned information to a new situation. Emotionally she presented the picture of a tense, fearful, withdrawn child who is prone to emotional outbursts.

An educational therapy program was constructed specifically focusing on reading, and including the development of a sound-symbol relationship. She entered a program consisting primarily of the S.R.A. *Dystar* reading material. The therapist also worked with Tina to help her develop a vocabulary and to apply factual information learned in one situation to problems encountered in another.

We worked with Tina for three months and found that she was making considerable gains. However, toward the end of this three month period it appeared that Tina had hit a plateau and no longer was progressing. She displayed a defeated attitude and had emotional outbursts. The mother reported to the therapist that for some unexplained reason family discord had developed—particularly with the two younger daughters who were beginning to "pick on" Tina. She also reported a general breakdown in family communication and functioning as exhibited by rebellion centered around household duties and other responsibilities such as homework.

Our staff discussed Tina and the family situation, and it was felt that the behavior of the other children was important and that something more than a learning problem was involved in this family. The mother was counseled and family therapy was suggested. The family agreed and we began a series of 11 conjoint sessions with two of these conducted in the home. The family sessions were conducted by the author and Tina's educational therapist, who acted as co-therapist. During the first two sessions it became apparent that the two sisters were very angry with Tina, rejecting and not including her in their activities with friends in the neighborhood. Tina was seen as the dummy or "monkey" of the family. The other girls had assumed roles for themselves. Cher was the good student, getting A's in school, quiet, studious, and tending to her own business. Sonny was the socialite of the family, but also was a good student. Both roles were in the success direction, unlike Tina's role in the family, in school and in the neighborhood.

During the fourth session a discussion was entered into with the mother as to which of the three children were like her. She promptly responded that *Tina was* and then followed a discussion of the mother's adolescence and social problems at that time. It became apparent in following sessions that the mother was anxious for Tina to do well in school, and had placed considerable pressure on her through social expectations. The other two girls felt isolated and excluded and had developed their roles as good student and socialite—their way of bidding for mother's attention. It also was apparent that the mother had placed Tina in a double bind by saying to her, "I want you to get better" but "if you do I will withdraw my attention from you and ignore you as I have your sisters."

What seemed to be happening prior to the family sessions was that Tina had begun to show improvement and her mother therefore expressed pleasure. This was a threat to the other two girls, Sonny and Cher, who acted out to maintain the status quo. The therapist and co-therapist pointed this out to the family members and worked toward family communication of a much more direct nature. As part of this process, the mother was helped to organize household chores and responsibilities, making use of positive reinforcement techniques, primarily contingency management. This helped to reduce the amount of nagging and verbalization that the mother had engaged in as a response to the girls' rebelliousness.

The two sessions held in the home were very productive. These were the fourth and the final sessions. It was during the fourth session that Sonny and Cher displayed anxiety and revealed how they were desperately trying to maintain roles as good student and socialite to keep themselves in mother's pleasure. The mother was helped directly to deal with her own feelings of isolation and exclusion which occurred during her adolescence and she was able to maintain a separation of her previous emotional problems and what was happening with Tina. During the seventh or eighth family session Tina again spurted ahead in her academic competency and this development continued after family sessions were terminated. She now has been discharged from the Center and is functioning in reading and math approximately one grade level below placement. This is felt to be appropriate for her general mental ability.

BARRY

Barry Knowles first came to the Center at the chronological age of 9 years and 10 months. He was referred by the school psychologist who stated:

"Barry has constantly displayed a deficient attitude toward all aspects of school and disciplinary measures. He deliberately antagonizes other children and denies any wrongdoing. Barry has good conversational ability; however, he seems willing only to share his experiences and knowledge with the teacher. He does not communicate well with other students. He has little self-discipline in any area. He has a violent temper which he cannot control."

The teacher reported that he reads at a primer level and his math is at a low second grade level. Barry was evaluated by a pediatrician and diagnosed as having minimal cerebral dysfunction. Ritilin was prescribed, but proved ineffective, so Barry was referred to our Center.

School History

Barry's school history indicates that his progress in kindergarten and first grade was average. It was during the second grade that problems emerged. These centered about difficulties in all skill areas and the development of behavior problems, primarily involving hyperactivity, distractability, and rebelliousness.

Developmental History

Barry's developmental history is unremarkable in that his birth and developmental progress appeared to be normal. He showed no difficulties in the first year of life. At 13 months he became very dehydrated due to a high fever and was hospitalized for one week. From 13 months to 8 years of age Barry was in and out of the hospital four or five times with bronchitis and asthma.

Family

Barry's family consists of Barry, his mother and father. Mr. Knowles has been confined in a wheelchair since he was 11 due to a nerve disease which has affected his lower extremities. This condition is not progressive. He is now manager of a trailer park and there is a moderately stable income. Mrs. Knowles works with her husband in the trailer park; she does most of the bookkeeping plus any chores made impossible by her husband's disability. The parents have been married for 12 years. They report no significant emotional problems, marital or otherwise. They view Barry's problem as centering about his behavior. However, the mother does admit that she has been yelling at Barry for a considerable time but that it has seemed ineffective.

Test Results

Barry was given a series of psychological and educational tests. On the *Wechsler Intelligence Scale for Children* he received a Verbal Scale IQ of 111, a Performance Scale IQ of 107, and Full Scale IQ of 110. On the *Wide Range Achievement Test* he obtained a Reading score of 2.7, Spelling of 2.6 and Arithmetic of 2.8. His performance on the *Bender Visual Motor Gestalt Test* was suggestive of mild neurological impairment with several rotations, collisions, and distortions. Barry had several learning problems. In arithmetic he had difficulties in column addition, simple multiplication, and addition with carrying. He had difficulty in short- and long-term memory. His handwriting showed incorrect cursive letter formation and some reversals. Reading was characterized by substitutions, a poor sight vocabulary, and a weak sound-symbol relationship. Emotional behavior was characterized by hyperactivity, distractability, defiant attitude, denial, temper tantrums, impulsivity, and very few internal controls with an active fantasy life. Barry thus presented a classic picture of a hyperactive child with minimal cerebral dysfunction.

He was started on an educational therapy program working directly with letter formation, word and letter sound-symbol relationships, and simple arithmetic processes. He also was involved in a visual-motor perceptual training program. Due to the behavior problems and the anxieties of the parents we involved this family in a family therapy program from the beginning. Six conjoint sessions were conducted, all in the Center, with the author as therapist.

The first three sessions were devoted to working through the parents' anger toward Barry and their tendency to describe his behavior and then throw up their hands in frustration. A behavior modification program was instituted, centered primarily about a warning system in which Barry's unacceptable behavior was acknowledged by the parent who would hold up one finger. If Barry did not immediately cease the inappropriate behavior, two fingers were held up, and Barry then was banished to his room. This had some immediate effect and succeeded in calming the family to a point where we could discuss relationships.

Mr. Knowles played a passive role and did not support his wife in attempts to deal with Barry. This was related to his intense desire that Barry have all the advantages that were denied the father due to physical disability. Mr. Knowles wished Barry "to be a man" and was giving tacit permission for him to act out and to engage in hyperactive behavior. Mrs. Knowles did not understand her husband or Barry and felt trapped and isolated from both. This was pointed out to the mother and father. Mr. Knowles began to deal with feelings about his physical disability, and at this point it was discovered that no one ever had talked to Barry about his father's condition.

Barry had developed an intense fantasy that his father's disability was progressive, that he was going to die, and the family would be abandoned. Once this was expressed and talked about in a direct manner, Barry experienced an obvious sense of relief. As family communication improved and the father was able to support the mother, Barry's hyperactivity decreased remarkably and the behavior modification program became even more effective. His functioning in remedial activities at the Center took a sharp upturn, and the school reported that he no longer was the behavioral problem he had been. Barry still is in educational therapy, but it is expected that he will terminate in another month or so.

References

Bateman, B., (Ed.) (1971). *Learning Disorders,* Seattle: Special Child Publications.

Burton, A. (Ed.) (1969). *Encounter, the Theory and Practice of Encounter Groups,* San Francisco: Jossey-Bass.

Dreikurs, R. (1968). *Psychology in the Classroom,* New York: Harper and Row.

Dreikurs, R., and Soltz, V. (1964). *Children: The Challenge,* New York: Duell, Sloan & Pearce.

Friedman, A.S., Broxzormenyi-Nagy, I., Jungreis, J.E., Lincoln, G., Mitchell, H.E., Sonne, J.C., Speek, R.V., and Spivak, G. (1968). *Psychotherapy for the Whole Family,* New York: Springer.

Furman, E. (1950). "Treatment of under fives by way of their parents," in *The Psychoanalytic Study of the Child,* vol. 12, New York: International Universities Press.

Gordon, T. (1970). *Parent Effectiveness Training: The 'No-Lose' Program for Raising Responsible Children*, New York: Peter H. Wyden.

Guerney, B.J., Jr. (1964). "Filial therapy: description and rationale," *Journal of Consulting Psychology, 28,* 304–310.

Hill, L.B. (1955). *Psychotherapeutic Intervention in Schizophrenia*, Chicago: University of Chicago Press.

Jackson, D.D. (Ed.) (1968). *Communication, Family and Marriage*, Palo Alto, Calif.: Science and Behavior Books.

Mathis, H.I. (1971). "Training a 'disturbed' boy using the mother as therapist: A case study," *Behavior Therapy, 2,* 233–239.

Patterson, G.R., Ray, R.S. and Shaw, D.A. (1968). "Direct intervention in families of deviant children," *Oregon Research Institute Bulletin, 9.*

Perls, F.S. (1969). *Gestalt Therapy Verbatim*, Walnut Creek, Calif.: Real People Press.

Rosenthal, R. (1968). "Self fulfilling prophecy," *Psychology Today, 2,* (Sept.), 44–51.

Satir, V. (1967). *Conjoint Family Therapy: A Guide to Theory and Technique*, Palo Alto, Calif.: Science and Behavior Books.

Walcher, L.O., Kohen, S.J., Breiter, D.E., Daston, P.G., Hirsch, I.S., and Leibowitz, J.M. (1969). "Teaching behavioral principles to parents of disturbed children," in B.J. Guerney, Jr. (Ed.), *Psychotherapeutic Agents, New Roles for Non-Professionals, Parents and Teachers*, New York: Holt, Rinehart and Winston, 443–449.

Related Reading

Family Treatment

Ackerman, N.W. (1958). *The Psychodynamics of Family Life*, New York: Basic Books.

Ackerman, N.W. (1962). "Family psychotherapy and psychoanalysis: Implications of difference," *Family Process, 1,* 30–43.

Boszormenyi-Nagy, I., and Framo, J.L., (Eds.) (1965). *Intensive Family Therapy: Theoretical and Practical Aspects*, New York: Hoeber Medical Division, Harper and Row.

Friedman, A.S. (1962). "Family therapy as conducted in the home," *Family Process, 1,* 132–145.

Friedman, A.S., Boszormenyi-Nagy, I., Jungreis, J.E., Lincoln G., Mitchell, H.E., Sonne, J.C., Speek, R.V. and Spivak, G. (1965) *Psychotherapy For The Whole Family*, New York: Springer Publishing Co., Inc.

Grossberg, J.M. (1964). "Behavior therapy: a review," *Psychological Bulletin 62,* 73–88.

Haley, J. (1962). "Whither family therapy?" *Family Process, 1,* 69–103.

Haley, J., and Hoffman, L. (1967). *Techniques of Family Therapy*, New York: Basic Books.

Hawkins, R.P., Peterson, R.F., Schweid, E., and Bijou, S.W. (1967). "Behavior therapy in the home: Amelioration of problem parent-child relations with a parent in a therapeutic role," *Journal of Experimental Child Psychology, 4,* 99–107.

Jackson, D.D., and Weakland, J.H. (1961). "Conjoint family therapy, some considerations on theory, technique and results," *Psychiatry, 24,* 30–45.

Jackson, D.D. (Ed.) (1968) *Communication, Family and Marriage,* Palo Alto, Calif.: Science and Behavior Books.

MacGregor, R.A., Ritchie, A.M., *et al.* [*1964*]. *Multiple Impact Therapy with Families,* New York: McGraw-Hill.

Watzlawick, P. (1966). "A structured family interview," *Family Process, 5,* 256–271.

Precision and Operant Methods

Bandura, A. (1969). *Principles of Behavior Modification,* New York: Holt, Rinehart, and Winston.

Gassholt, M. (1970). "Precision techniques in the management of teacher and child behaviors," *Exceptional Children, 37,* 129–136.

Glavin, J.P., Quay, H.C., Annesly, F.R., and Werry, J.S. (1971). "An experimental resource room for behavior problem children," *Exceptional Children, 38,* 131–137.

Graubard, P.S. (1969). "Utilizing the group in teaching disturbed delinquents to learn;" *Exceptional Children, 36,* 267–272.

Meacham, M.C., and Wiesen, A.L. (1969). *Changing Classroom Behavior: A Manual for Precision Teaching,* Scranton: International Textbook.

Patterson, G.R. (1969). "The mother as a social engineer in the classroom," in J. Krumboltz and C. Thoreson (Eds.), *Behavior Counseling: Cases and Techniques,* New York: Holt, Rinehart and Winston

Patterson, G.R., and Gullion, M.E. (1968). *Living with Children: New Methods for Parents and Teachers,* Champaign, Ill.: Research Press.

Quay, H.C., Werry, J.S., McQueen, M., and Sprague, R.L. (1966). "Remediation of the conduct problem child in the special class setting," *Exceptional Children, 32,* 509–575.

Woody, R.H. (1966). "Behavior therapy and school psychology," *Journal of School Psychology, 4,* 1–14.

CHAPTER 10

Jerry - A Case of Behavior Disorder

WILLIAM V. BURLINGAME

Editor's Introduction

Jerry is an example of a youth type that arouses public attention and anxiety. Delinquent and marginally involved in a counterculture, he reminds us of the remarkably uneven flow between contemporary generations. He elicits uneasiness and resentment in parents who are unable to transmit skills and values and in teachers who find most of their energy consumed in maintaining order.

The deviant is most strongly noted if he challenges or threatens the social order. Indeed, that attention is often an added stimulus to making threats or creating disorder. Youthful delinquents trigger a special quality of attention, perhaps because youthful misbehavior pricks the conscience of adults or because youth will shape the future or because youth have newly acquired a significant economic, social and political power.

A shift toward a massive and metropolitan society was accompanied by alienation, more apparent dependency, increased antagonism toward established goals and methods in school, and violence without intense anger. The "opportunity theory" or compensation for lack of opportunity falls short in explaining the change from delinquency as a neighborhood phenomenon to a general social problem. There are obvious social determinants, rewards, and compensations for these behaviors and some of the growth in delinquency is an artifact of changes in case-finding and recording. Nevertheless, specific disorders cannot be separated from individual factors. Drugs, violence, and delinquency may serve as a tranquilizer for loneliness, a counteraction for aimlessness or a shield for vulnerability.

The following case report makes *self* something *more than a reflection of society.* It fits with findings that specific misconduct is related to the situation but also to ego strength and the level of moral concept development (Kohlberg, 1966). What happens in a given place, at a given time, or under specific circumstances, inevitably possesses a quality of that place or moment or circumstance, but it contains also some inner formula for action. The point of view at John Umstead Hospital, Adolescent Unit is neo-analytic, using ego-psychology more than id-psychology (Brochure, John Umstead Hospital, 1971). In that model, ego development underlies the push toward reality testing and mastery, the defining of self and the integration of experience (Bower, 1966).

Ego growth is hindered in barren and stressful environments, and damaged by defects in parental warmth and communication. Almost universally, research supports the view that referrals to children's clinics are most prevalent from conflict dominated families (Becker and Iwakami, 1969), and likewise, a sample of disturbed children will have an atypical number of neurotic or psychotic mothers (Brodie and Winterbottom, 1967). Most parents use temporary withdrawal of love as a technique for control or socialization of children. Such a technique is destructive, ambiguous, or meaningless where love is malformed or meager.

Strong conscience grows in a warm family, and ego with conscience comes from a joining of love and reason.

Jerry is an example of child disturbance related to family "illness," a case of problems interwoven. Each member responds only at the level of personal defense. Mrs. Glover had a difficult relation with her own father; she feels inferior and unworthy. The Glovers were not eager to have a child. The birth brought problems of illness, fatigue, and conflict with neighbors. Parents so uncertain of identity, so anxious to prove themselves, and so beset with problems of management can scarcely be a gratifying and reliable guide for ego growth.

At long last Jerry arrives in a therapeutic milieu. Fortunately it is one which can tolerate the heightened misbehavior that occurs in early weeks and the regressions that occur much later. This is an unusual public facility willing to undertake sophisticated and long-term care. In many settings the acting out patient simply "does not last."

The Adolescent Unit serves 12 boys and 12 girls, with another 26 in the school. Admission follows an evaluation in the Childrens Psychiatric Institute. This process requires a week or 10 days, with the child either outpatient or living-in while parents commute. Treatment includes:

- individual psychotherapy, two per week with a non-administrative therapist;
- instruction, range fron one-to-one to six-to-one (treatment related);
- milieu, recreation and living structured to treatment; and
- parent counseling, mandatory, emphasizing contemporary matters (Brochure, 1971).

Emphasis is placed on "corrective experience" in relation with other patients and staff, on talking our more than acting out, and using a relatively open setting to:
1. understand feelings and behavior,

2. gain in both capacity and desire to control behaviors, to manage rather than be controlled by them,
3. find and practice more effective means of securing gratification.

A program of this sort is ordinarily attentive to the idea that failure separates and isolates the child who becomes increasingly guarded, deceptive and withdrawn. It is necessary to increase communication, the response to social reinforcement, and identification with models (Brendtro, 1969). Diagnoses, finding an etiology, and decoding day-to-day behavior give direction to treatment, but the client must also engage in new ideas and experiences with people who are not easily incorporated into the pathology—rather who are reliable, intense, and caring over a significant period.

THE STRUCTURE OF ADOLESCENT DELINQUENCY

"Jerry" may be viewed as a composite whose personality development does not fit easily into diagnostic categories or popular etiological explanations. Commonly, such youngsters are called "delinquent," a quasi-legal or sociological term emphasizing the deviant and antisocial nature of their deeds; dated diagnostic manuals include the "psychopath" and "sociopath" sobriquets which call attention to defective conscience development, the failure to inculcate proper values, the inclination to ignore convention, mores, and statute, and a cavalier disregard for the rights, feelings, or property of others, all seemingly occurring without remorse or guilt. Other nomenclatures refer to the "impulse ridden" or "impulse discharge" personality, thus underscoring the difficulty these individuals have in tolerating stress and frustration, and their propensity to gratify needs in short order and without the mediating strictures of conscience. Most commonly employed are the terms "character disorder" and "acting out," labels which recognize the common factor of behavioral difficulty which is manifest in transactions with society.

In the lives of such adolescents, the criterion behaviors are conspicuous: usually there is a level of school achievement lower than academic ability would predict and it declines with increasing age; by the junior high years there is school truancy, suspensions and expulsions; there is long-standing, bitter, and intense conflict with figures of authority (parents, teachers, principals, the police, and supervisors in general), the contested entity being the possession of power and authority; experimentation and routine usage of a variety of drugs, with alcohol, marijuana, hashish, and LSD being the most frequent, is nearly universal; sexual promiscuity, i.e., nearly indiscriminate sexual activity may occur, particularly among girls; numbers of these adolescents have had several runaway episodes, most commonly from home, but also from boarding schools and military academies where some have been placed in the attempt to supply firmer controls over their behavior. Significant proportions of these activities occur in concert with other adolescents. It is, for example, common for runaways, school truancy, and drug abuse to happen in pairs and small groups. This observation led sociologists of earlier days to identify the delinquent gang phenomenon, but it would be erroneous to assume that the antisocial behavior is exclusively the product of the group rather than that of individual motivation. Furthermore, the relationships in the delinquent groups are often scarcely more fruitful than those with adults; the same patterns of disloyalty, suspicion, self-centeredness, and anger interfere. What binds these adolescents together is often little more than sharing the common enemy of adult authority and the same pursuit of gratification and impulse discharge. The capacity to give and to share, and the reciprocity which characterizes more mature relationships is conspicuously absent.

Other behavior, which is the logical extension of that previously cited, may also exist. Shoplifting and vandalism are common, as is fighting among these boys, especially in their younger years. In recent years, visible alternative subcultures or countercultures have developed and have provided both refuge and protective coloration for vast numbers of behavior disordered teen-agers. The abandonment of more traditional values, the emphasis on contemporary experience, and the highlighting of the pleasure principle have made for a fairly comfortable articulation, particularly with the so-called hippie culture.

It can be seen that this rather loosely defined group with

its rebellious anger, impulsivity, and inclination toward abrasive contact with others is dramatically different from those with other varieties of emotional disturbance. We are speaking here of conflict between the individual and society which is quite apart from "neurotic" conflict, in which various components or agents of a single personality are said to be engaged in "conflict," producing such symptoms as anxiety, depression, fatigue, or psychosomatic illness. Both the aforementioned are to be distinguished from "psychosis," in which ties with reality may be lost, in which there is significant withdrawal, and where an inner, autistic world may be substituted for external reality.

THE DEVELOPMENT OF SERIOUS PROBLEMS

At age 15 Jerry was reluctantly committed to the Department of Mental Health in his state by the psychiatrist who worked with him. Over several weeks there had been a number of unproductive psychotherapeutic interviews and it became apparent that the rising crescendo of acting out was certain to carry him into court again, and eventually into the juvenile correctional system. The report prepared by Jerry's psychiatrist included the following observations:

> I saw Jerry for six therapy sessions; then he failed to keep the seventh appointment. It was during this time that his behavior deteriorated rapidly and I was fearful that he would soon be arrested or come into contact with legal authorities in some other unfortunate fashion. In summary, emotional arrangement in terms of impulse control, frustration tolerance, and judgment are seriously defective. He indulges in magical wishful thinking, is hedonistically oriented, and is defective in superego development. He formed warm rapport with me, but on a very superficial level, and would like me as long as I would protect him or give in to his desires. Loyalty or affection is unknown to him and he is remarkably able to give up one emotional relationship for another. The relationship with his parents is extremely poor. I feel strongly that he is incapable of utilizing psychotherapy as an out-patient, and requires definitive institutional treatment within a structured environment for years to come. He must be away from the family where the relationship has been so disturbed for so many years. His main strengths are his superior intelligence (IQ: 125), the lack of viciousness, his charm and appeal, and physical attractiveness. The work with him is apt to be prolonged and difficult.

The police eventually apprehended Jerry at the home of an older boy whose history included drug use and sales, charges of contributing to the delinquency of a minor, and a lengthy series of confrontations with family and school. A planned runaway to a Florida beach town was foiled and Jerry was transported to a security ward of the state hospital. His initial rage was immense and although he trembled and seemed about to lash out physically at hospital admitting personnel, he restricted himself to verbal abuse directed equally toward his father, who had betrayed him for the "last time", and the psychiatrist whom he had made the error of "trusting."

In a few days Jerry cooled somewhat and began to provide an account of the struggle occuring between him and his parents. When asked why he had been committed, he responded: "I started standing up to my father . . . The time for him to tell me what to do and for me to say, 'Yes, Sir', is gone; I need a reason." Chronologically, Jerry dated the decline of the relationship with his parents to an event which occurred in the fifth grade and which was singularly important because it was the first time he had "really disobeyed." There was an argument with his mother over which shoes to wear to school, with Jerry demanding to be allowed to wear his tennis shoes and mother insisting on a pair of oxfords. Even at 10 years of age he was sensitive to the fact that tennis shoes had greater status value among fifth grade boys, the implication being that as the relationships with his parents became unsatisfying, he had turned prematurely to his peers for affection and acceptance. Jerry's mother hid the tennis shoes and Jerry refused to go to school that day. There was a whipping when his father came home from work and the pattern was established for the numerous beatings which would occur over the next five years: his father would conspicuously remove his belt, corner Jerry, beat him vigorously, and then lecture sternly. In later years, the beatings assumed the proportions of sadistic assault as both the mother and father would be required, one to restrain him physically while the other beat. On Jerry's part, there were feelings of humiliation and hate, and he refused to cry, no matter how great the pain, in order to deprive the parents of the satisfaction of knowing he was hurt. In addition, he concluded that they must hate him or they could not have treated him so savagely and unfeelingly. Superseding all other feelings, however, was the determination to retaliate, to demonstrate that such unfairness would not go unanswered.

The sixth grade witnessed deficits in self-control on the playground as Jerry would lose his temper, swear, and be punished. This led to "cutting up" in the classroom, sojourns in the principals' office, more punishment, and spiteful retaliation. In an attempt to get Jerry to raise his grades, the father offered either a deep sea fishing trip or a vacation to Washington, D.C.; Jerry decided that he had no interest in fishing and could find no reason to go to Washington. By age 12 the estrangement was sufficiently acute that incentive plans with positive options were declined.

The next move was to substitute unattractive alternatives in the hope of extracting school performance and obedience as the lesser of two painful situations: due to his failure to perform in the sixth grade, Jerry was forced to attend summer school. He was furious and decided to "buck everything." It was not long before the teacher provided a pretext for Jerry's anger. After she failed to announce recess, he swore at her and was subsequently sent home, and his parents sentenced him to three days of yard work as punishment. The struggle was now full-blown with moves and countermoves well established and with no party able to withdraw from the contest. There were Jerry's crimes and transgressions which precipitated punishment, pain, and humiliation, followed by retaliation from Jerry which led to more savage and seemingly sadistic reprisal, thus setting the scene for another round. By the beginning of the seventh grade there was critical estrangement and alienation, and Jerry began to turn to other troubled adolescents in the hope of securing the support and respect he could not gain at home. The events of the next three years served only to enhance and escalate the conflict, to rupture nearly beyond repair the already defective dependency bond between him and his parents, to increase the anger and bitterness, and to debilitate further his faulty self-esteem.

In the seventh grade, Jerry went underground, due in large part to fear of his father. He sniped, undermined, and harassed, but maintained a superficial facsimile of compliance, while displacing his abundant anger through acting out at school. At home they argued over the length of his hair and the style of his clothes, with Jerry feeling that his parents could afford the clothes he wanted and that he should be permitted to regulate the length of his hair. The father emphasized what was "proper" and there were forced visits to the barber shop, choices offered between haircuts and beatings, and brief runaway episodes when the day of the haircut occurred. A broken leg during the summer between the seventh and the eighth grade effectively reduced Jerry's mobility and resulted in several months of relative quiescence.

In the eighth grade Jerry resumed the struggle with redoubled fury. On Christmas eve and Christmas night he sneaked out his window and drank beer with a friend; he recalls being in bed after he had returned and phrasing a response to his father: "I'm going to keep doing things until you give up trying to tell me what to do." For the next several months, the campaign was deliberate and provocative as he went out on school nights, frequented pool halls, flirted with drugs and liquor, all of which served as a catalyst for the inevitable arguments and physical punishment. Hair remained an issue, with Jerry concluding, "If he can tell me to cut my hair, he can tell me to do anything."

By spring the parents could tolerate the situation no longer and his father took matters to the juvenile court. Jerry was placed on probation with a number of conditions—that he obey his parents, obey at school, refrain from drinking, participate in group therapy at the mental health clinic, and stay out of pool halls. Jerry was enraged, convinced that his influential lawyer father had manipulated the court to enforce by legal means what he had been unable to secure by physical force and threat. In his fury, Jerry set out to break each of the conditions of probation in conspicuous and public fashion. His newly achieved delinquent status was an additional weapon and he employed it to embarass his father in the business community. Jerry immediately ceased performing at school (thus failing the eighth grade) and indulged in such reprisals as stealing his father's liquor ("so I could say I broke two of the rules at one time and at his expense"). When matters again reached critical proportions, his father sought the court's intervention. Jerry spent a week in the juvenile detention facility, and under duress from the court, chose to repeat the eighth grade in a military academy in preference to reform school.

Again, Jerry was infuriated, seeing only his father's controlling and manipulating, but having no perspective on the self-defeating nature of his own deeds. In his rage, Jerry spent that autumn writing letters home and making collect phone calls whose sole content was some brief but stinging obscenity. His feelings were visited on the military academy as one might suspect: he ran away, amassed a record number of demerits, and, in general, replicated the circular process of misdemeanor, punishment, retaliation, accelerated punishment, enhanced fury, and so forth. He eventually responded to the threat of reform school, completed the eighth grade, and returned home. Shortly afterward Jerry resumed drinking, staying out late, and, in addition, picked up with a new group of questionable companions. No more than a month after he had returned from the military academy, he was charged with breaking and entering, although the motive was not larceny or simple burglary as much as the attempt to find liquor and a vacant house where he and his companions could consume it.

At this juncture, with Jerry almost continuously away from home, the recently consulted psychiatrist arranged for mandatory hospitalization. Jerry himself seemed almost to sense the futility of it all; following the runaway to Florida, he anticipated returning to face the breaking and entering charge, and if not institutionalized, he hoped to secure permission to live with his friend and return to school. Regarding his father, he mused, "I was even tired of disobeying." The struggle and the anger eclipsed and submerged most other aspects of Jerry's life. There were, however, some other features of note which were more than marginally significant to him. In the process of disavowing the relationship with his parents, he turned to his contemporaries for emotional sustenance. His quickness to anger, the erratic impulsive quality, the self-centeredness, and his preoccupation with battling authority interfered; he had few friends and focused instead on acquiring the superficial vendors of status which included long hair, stylized clothing, and daring deeds. His efforts were not particularly successful and Jerry occasionally experienced genuine sadness or depression before some impulsive outbreak contrived to obscure the underlying loneliness. Similarly, he reached out to girls and suffered what he interpreted to be cataclysmic rejection which again precipitated feelings of depression.

JERRY'S FAMILY AND CHILDHOOD

It can be seen that the decline which occurred between years 10 and 15 was gradual at the outset but picked up sufficient momentum to become virtually irreversible in later years. Each insult was cumulative in nature, but no single event was critically traumatic. How the poisonous climate—in which corrective or healing functions were so completely absent—could develop can be inferred from examining Jerry's family and his earlier years. The parents, Mr. and Mrs. Glover, were married when the father finished law school. Mrs. Glover had scarcely completed the emancipation from her own family and had endured a most difficult relationship with her father. Although she had done well in school and had striven to achieve the status of model child, her efforts were never sufficient; it seemed as if she were always found lacking and inadequate. Throughout childhood and into her adult years, she harbored chronic feelings of inferiority and unworthiness together with the constant apprehension that she would one day be overwhelmed by life's trials and the demands of others. In addition, there was her own abundant anger and resentment, readily available for expression toward Jerry and his father when she perceived them draining her of strength and resource.

Mr. Glover, on the other hand, was a testimony to the merits of such virtues as sacrifice, deferred gratification, and hard work. He was a child of a poor family during the Depression and had achieved successful professional status with little parental help. The inflexible dedication to work, his attitudes regarding self-denial, the over-valuing of middle class status and its symbols, and the rigid insistence on self-control, while conducive to economic success and upward social class mobility, were not necessarily concomitant with successful child rearing.

From the beginning there were difficulties; the pregnancy was not planned and caught both parents by surprise only three months after marriage at a time when they felt they could ill afford to begin a family. The pregnancy and delivery were uncomplicated, however. Such was not the case with the first 18 months of life, during which time Jerry was hospitalized twice (for a severe respiratory infection and a subsequent tonsillectomy) and suffered considerably with earaches, colic, and an allergic reaction to milk. Infant Jerry cried and ultimately the Glovers were forced to change apartments following repeated complaints from other tenants; the parents acknowledge a thinly suppressed anger toward their firstborn at that time. Hardly had the several physical problems been resolved when toilet training was initiated, and for 20 months Jerry strenuously resisted his mother's efforts. To Jerry's seemingly intentional "accidents" with his sphincters, to the jealousy expressed toward a younger brother who was born when he was 30 months old, and to his propensity to escape from the yard and investigate the neighborhood, the mother responded with a regimen of increasing anger and repeated spankings. Jerry's earliest recollections (which are corroborated by the parents) are of the later preschool years when he remembers searching for food throughout the neighborhood and of subsequent spankings when his mother found him. The effect and meaning of such early events must remain speculative; it is clear, however, that this child, in his neediness, triggered his mother's impatience and set the scene for the frustration of his dependency needs, with ensuing rage from the child, and a fierce battle for autonomy and control. Whether the early separations through hospitalization substantially interfered with mothering, whether the battle around toilet training was the prototype for all subsequent machinations with authority, and whether the search for food at age 4 represented the pursuit of dependency outside the family, cannot be determined. At the least, these events may not have been critical *per se,* but were instrumental in setting a course which ultimately led to psychiatric hospitalization when Jerry was 15.

The first four years of school seemed reasonably successful, but the harbingers of later and much graver difficulty were present in the form of teachers' comments in the cumulative record: His first grade teacher noted that he had difficulty "concentrating" and "applying himself" for any period of time; the second grade teacher spoke of "his insistence that everything go his way"; the third grade teacher listed the same items but added that "he resents being corrected"; it was the fourth grade teacher who described him as "intellectually able", but stated that "he must learn to control his temper." Jerry himself remembers being reprimanded as early as the first grade. Trips to the principal's office were fairly common by the fourth grade, at which time his grades began to fall. His acting out seemed aimed at

securing notice from other children and was rather imper-
sonally directed at teacher authority. He describes liking
some of his teachers in the primary grades, but acting out
nonetheless when they would leave the classroom or when
he could get someone else to participate with him.

THE HOSPITAL AND ADOLESCENT UNIT

Jerry, at age 15, was scarcely a cooperative patient. He had
been apprehended by the police and transported very much
against his wishes to a closed ward of a state mental hospital.
The fact that this event was an alternative to, and precluded
his placement in jail or reform school was of no consequence. The sole consideration weighing with him was the
current insult to his autonomy and the resulting anger which
now sought an outlet. He had no awareness of his own role
in precipitating and perpetuating the present disaster, nor
any way of appraising the extent of his anger and the generally self-defeating course of events which he pursued. He
viewed his hospitalization as one further incident in the
struggle with his father. The only benefit he saw was the
likelihood that the breaking and entering charge would be
dropped in view of his new status as "mental patient." Otherwise he saw no reason for this latest incarceration and assumed that with "good behavior" he would be released
within a month.

The need for prolonged treatment was related to him and
he was transferred to the hospital's adolescent service where
this could be undertaken. It was evident, however, that there
was considerable discrepancy between Jerry's perceptions
and those of the treatment staff. His transfer to the adolescent service represented the opportunity for greater freedom
and for contact with other teen-agers; he did not share the
staff's belief that he required lengthy treatment. Jerry was
fortunate that his state supports an Adolescent Unit which
specializes in the intensive residential treatment of selected,
seriously troubled teen-agers. This program, which accom-
modates 24 boys and girls, includes individual psychotherapy, parent counseling, special education, recreation, structured group life, and the necessary physical facilities.*

It was not long before Jerry's feelings began to emerge and

*The Adolescent Unit, John Umstead Hospital, Butner, North Carolina, a
facility of the North Carolina Department of Mental Health.

bring him into repeated conflict with the Unit's authority structure. In psychotherapy, he described his hate and contempt for the counselors (the child care staff who supervise the living areas) and his resentment of the teachers. With whatever flimsy rationalizations he could contrive, he managed to be angry, provocative, and resistive, and to view those countermeasures that the staff would muster as evidence of their arbitrariness, stupidity, or malice toward him, which might then justify his anger. It was, of course, the same cyclical conflict as had occurred in the family, and it required most careful handling for the staff to avoid being construed by Jerry as punitive, vengeance-seeking adults. Had he been able to provoke the treatment staff to a sufficient degree, it would have been quite possible for Jerry to maintain his distorted perceptions and to view the anger as external to himself. Over the early months of treatment, the counselors recorded incident after incident of Jerry's negativism and provocation:

12-4: This evening Jerry Glover seemed to be the center of acting up which went on until bedtime. The boys were loud and picked on Mark until I had to separate him from the group. When I did this, Jerry led the clapping, whistling, and jeering which was directed at me.

12-8: Both Jerry and Steve have been cutting up all day and were finally secluded until tomorrow morning. On the ward this morning both boys were hollering and yelling frequently and using vulgar language. When called down about this, they ignored me. Finally, both were told that any similar outburst would cause them to be secluded. At lunch they started yelling at some of the elderly patients from other Units. When we returned to the Unit, these two boys were secluded.

12-13: Jerry Glover's privileges were taken for two days as a result of throwing crackers on the floor and not cleaning them up when asked to do so. He adamantly refused to pick up the crackers and was talking back and cussing the whole time. When told that his privileges would be taken he said that he didn't care if they were taken for a month because his therapist would give them back when he is seen again.

12-18: Jerry was angry at being told to get up this morning. He wanted to argue with me over what happened Saturday night. He at first denied being part of it but after lengthy discussion he named off each incident he was involved in, stating, "We do stuff like this to get our anger out but mostly to see how confused we can make the counselors." He went on to say that he had been well behaved the past several days and saw nothing wrong in having a little "fun."

12–21:   Jerry, Steve, and Mike were throwing Ping-Pong paddles and chairs on the ward this morning and these same boys were throwing food, yelling, and cursing in the cafeteria. On returning to the ward they started throwing pillows and books. I had to seclude Mike and while I was involved in this, someone smashed a wooden chair to pieces. Jerry Glover seems to be starting most of the trouble. When asked why he was acting up, he stated that it was "fun to break things up" and "to confuse the counselors."

Jerry's teachers reported very similar behavior. For the week of December 10th, the entry is as follows:

Jerry has refused to work in math class all week, attempting to read in class or refusing to enter the room. In English, he "didn't feel like working" but was coaxed for two days and then blatantly refused on the third. He was accompanied to history class by a counselor on one day but then refused to enter the room. On Friday he worked in history but then announced that he would not abide by the new class schedule of meeting every day.

For the week of the seventeenth, the following was dictated:

Jerry came to history on Tuesday but refused to do anything; he sat and sulked while I carried on class with Jim. He missed a make-up test scheduled for that afternoon, didn't come to class on Wednesday, but told me that he wanted to make up the test on Friday when he thought he would be feeling better. This sounded like a diversionary tactic to me. In math, he seems to be playing hostile games by losing textbook after textbook. Other classes reveal the same sporadic attendance, refusal to participate, and general foot-dragging quality. There was considerable acting out during the field trip to the planetarium.

The single area of comparative success was psychotherapy where Jerry could rage on verbally about his alleged mistreatment and receive both sympathetic hearing and an opportunity for catharsis. He affiliated very quickly with his therapist whom he preceived as being on "his side," although the fragile relationship was severely tested almost daily. The therapist refused to extricate Jerry from the numerous difficulties in which he became embroiled, and insisted that Jerry himself had a significant role in creating them; these tactics and interpretations were tolerated but not well received. Repetitively over the winter months, the therapist pointed out Jerry's hostility and provocation, the self-defeating results, the lack of contemporary justification for his anger, the similarity of this current strife to previous situations, and the self-fulfilling quality in which he could usually justify his hostility by self-deception. Very gradually, the distortion was undone and Jerry could not longer rationalize his acting out or defend it on any logical basis. At that point, the anger began to diminish as did his acting out, only to be replaced by depression which he tolerated no better. Giving up the anger required years, but sufficient inroads were made so that, by the spring of his first year of treatment, he had become quieter, more reflective, and somewhat better controlled.

The feeling which alternated with anger was depression, as the sadness and loneliness resulting from years of interrupted nurturance began to be experienced rather than warded off or dissipated by acting out. Jerry had now been in treatment for approximately four months; the winter had been difficult for the staff as well as for him, but it was the depression which began to occur in the spring that he found intolerable. The treatment unit was located five miles from a major freeway, and 12 hours of productive hitchhiking could place one either in New York City or on Florida's beaches. Jerry began to run away, first to Florida and then to New York. He found the East Village and spent weeks in hippie street culture, living from crash pad to crash pad, begging on the streets for money, using drugs randomly, and searching for relationships which would remove the depression while not demanding excessively of him. Between the fifth and the eighth months of treatment, Jerry was absent from the Adolescent Unit for nearly as many days as he was present. Despite his alienation from the so-called "straight" society, Jerry found little promise in the hip culture. He would return from a runaway, railing at the disorder, the lack of personal cleanliness, the prevalence of hepatitis and venereal disease, and the disturbed thinking which he attributed to the effects of drug usage. The passivity and dependency associated with begging on the streets was noxious to his self-esteem and reawakened the feelings of helplessness and passivity which he had experienced in his family. He was troubled by the general purposelessness and aimlessness of life in the street culture, and, with his growing psychological sophistication, he was quick to spot the abundance of emotional disturbance, displaced anger, and psychopathy among its constituents. And so Jerry would return to the Adolescent Unit, depressed and chastened, having ruled out an alternative, but scarcely able to commit himself fully to the goals of the treatment program.

INTERPRETATION

Through the case of Jerry, the range of characteristics ordinarily associated with behavior disorder or character disorder has been illustrated. *It would be useful to examine a quintet of clinically recognizable features which is thought to be more or less present in this variety of personality disturbance,* to speculate regarding cause and effect, and to examine the interrelationships among such features.

First there is the visible acting out which consists of a rapid translation of impulse into action. There is very limited tolerance for frustration or delay of impulse, and the consequent behavior is called antisocial if tension reduction is secured at the expense of others. Such personalities are often characterized as hedonistic, impulse ridden, and narcissistic—terms which underscore the dedication to the reduction of stress and the enhancement of pleasure. How such personality defect develops requires use of the concept of deprivation, which assumes that there were critical deficits in early dependency relationships. Not only is the child making up for early losses, but it is believed that such deprivation has impaired the development of the capacity for impulse control. The personality is considered to be more vulnerable to internal and external stress.

Secondly, there exists a history of defective interpersonal relationships, with the individual relating to others in generally primitive ways. One sees excessive bids for attention and an incredible emotional neediness, with the demand that others provide gratification and that the balance of affectional trade always be in his favor. In extreme form the behavior disordered personality is shallow, untrustworthy, undependable, without loyalty, suspicious, and distrustful. Again, deficits in dependency gratification are responsible: personality is fixated at earlier primitive levels reflecting the failure to develop due to unmet need, with distrust and suspicion being heir to these early experiences with other human beings.

Third, there is the presence of depression, anxiety, and

anger in immense quantities. Existing often at less than conscious levels is profound depression, the result of the same ruptured dependency which had occurred comparatively early in life. The resulting loss is experienced as depression or sadness. One often sees frantic activity and excessive acting out whose purpose seems to be the relief or avoidance of acutely painful feelings; there is no question that one of the most common antecedents to drug and alcohol abuse and addiction is the use of these substances to relieve depressive affect. With only cursory examination of delinquents, the depression which is thought to be present may seem conspicuous by its absence. Still, there is the constant anxiety which seems related to the threatened breakthrough of unresolved depression, and the sadness itself often is not perceptible until such time as the activity and acting out are diminished by confinement in a hospital or correctional facility. The other prominent affect is anger which is the consequence of the same deprivation and loss. Any infringement can reawaken the original loss and anger can grow out of the feeling of being unjustly deprived, humiliated and disenfranchised. When others interfere in the pursuit of gratification or the reduction of stress, even when the outcome clearly will be disastrous, often there is further rage, together with a rigid, well defined system of defenses which prevents the individual from recognizing the unjustifiable, illogical, and irrational aspects of his behavior.

A *fourth* hallmark is the imperfect development of conscience and resulting distortions in the value system. If there is significant interference in early nurture, then it is not surprising to find that the child fails to "identify," i.e., to adopt and acquire parental values. This defect also might be viewed as the consequence of the child's failure to acquiese to the process of socialization: if he does not receive benefit, then there is no incentive to achieve self-control, to defer gratification to some more appropriate time, or to alter it to some more socially acceptable form. The issue of conscience is not an all or nothing matter, however. There are areas of value "numbness" and degrees of defect. The phenomenon of gang loyalty among delinquents illustrates that interpersonal loyalty may be present in some distorted form. Among a great many behavior disordered individuals there is also the "archaic superego," rigid, overly strict, guilt provoking incorporations which indicate that at some level the child also has accepted the blame and responsibility for the sad state of affairs. Perhaps he assumes that he must be at fault or they would not have neglected him, and, once having accepted this premise, the stage is set for guilt and self-punishment. It is the archaic superego which likely accounts for such apparently contradictory phenomena as acting out in order to be apprehended and punished, and the perfectionistic and puritanical qualities occasionally found in reformed delinquents and behavior disordered individuals who are undergoing treatment.

Finally, there are several defensive operations common to behavior disorder which serve to protect it from critical examination. Among the most frequently employed are "projection" and "denial," each of which operates to disguise the origin and meaning of angry affect and behavior. The behavior disordered child conveniently denies that the original act of aggression or unreasonable demand in each new transaction is his. All he experiences is the adult response which usually consists of retaliation, punishment, or the withdrawal of affection, and he thus feels justified in venting his anger. In like fashion, he can avoid taking responsibility for this behavior by "projecting" his own anger, that is, perceiving it as existing in the parent or adult instead. Phenomenologically, this child perceives the world as being angry with him rather than the converse. To summarize, each of the above features is related either directly or secondarily to failures in nurture. As has been suggested earlier, it is unlikely that there are single significant traumatic events, but rather, a lengthy process of deprivation and estrangement which has its origin in the early years of life.

The treatment and education of such children as Jerry is fraught with difficulty. At the outset, there is vigorous denial of the need for rehabilitative measures and an insistence that the plight is solely the product of adult malevolence. The stage is set for lengthy resistance and negativism. An additional complicating factor derives from the fact that the public schools, treatment units, and correctional facilities which house these youngsters are endowed with authority and must enforce behavioral limits and extract performance. The behavior disordered child is already hypersensitive to any such restrictions on his autonomy, and, no matter how reasonably applied, this exercise of power is likely to be resisted. The chronic behavioral difficulty inevitably leads to interrupted schooling and by the latter years of junior high there is usually substantial educational deficit, regardless of the level of intelligence. This educational loss, coupled with the child's impulsivity and limited tolerance for frustration, are additional factors which make continued, regular educational placement problematic. It is this group of adolescents which accounts for the greatest proportion of school drop-outs, suspensions, and expulsions.

Assuming that the hostility and resistance which are so abundant can be overcome, then what follows in the second phase is nearly as difficult to manage. There is depression and poor self-esteem which sap the initiative and contribute to an overall sense of futility. Working with this variety of disturbance presupposes a process in which the child becomes angry, refuses tasks, is discouraged, and gives up on many occasions. Several features must be present if successful treatment and rehabilitation are to occur. *Foremost* among these is the requirement that supportive and corrective relationships be established by teachers and child care personnel. The distrust and hostility can only be overcome when firmness is combined with warmth and support. The hostility and resistance are undone as the child becomes convinced that these significant adults are genuinely concerned about his plight. Establishing such support and correcting the life-long history of distrust is no easy or brief process; behavior disordered children are notoriously effective in sabotaging and corrupting the attempts of well-meaning adults by getting them to act out with them, by driving them away with their anger and resistance, and by seducing them into punitive counterattack, thus making any relationship impossible.

Secondly, there is the need for continuous feedback, for the interpretation of behavior, and for the processing of the endless behavioral incidents. While some of this might be done in formal psychotherapy, it is likely that the most effective work occurs in the classroom and living areas. The child must be confronted with his own provocation and anger in the attempt to undo the denial, projection, and avoidance of responsibility which follow as he plays out his feelings in the struggles with others.

Finally, there is the need for individualized educational planning and instruction for many behavior disordered children. The individual contact is one medium for the development of the corrective relationship which has been stressed. Aside from this, it is apparent that the poor self-esteem, limited tolerance for frustration, and educational deficits all demand greater provision for individual attention and one-to-one programming.

ELEMENTS OF SUCCESS

A postscript describing Jerry's subsequent treatment is of interest, considering that individuals with this variety of emotional disorder are least likely to remain in a voluntary program, and usually are last seen having dropped out or having been expelled from one facility or another. The work with Jerry was ultimately successful, in part because he was in compulsory treatment under court order, but also because the residential facility was sufficiently equipped to cope with his rage, resistance, and provocation. Although the first eight months were agonizing for the staff in this regard, the second phase of treatment was much more painful for him. When the acting out and running away were away were no longer tenable, Jerry began to invest himself in the rehabilitation program. He was in great distress from the depression that now washed over him with greater and greater intensity. It was relieved only by establishing relationships with others and Jerry lacked the skills to do this. He was frightened, did not know how to reach out, was disappointed, and felt let down when relationships failed to mature. He was inclined to elevate certain adults to heroic proportions, only to be disappointed when they failed to live up to expectations. It was during this second year of treatment that he would feel depressed or disappointed and would withdraw into silence, sleep, or reading for days and weeks at a time.

Inasmuch as he now had committed himself to his own treatment, disappointments were excruciating. Defeats came easily and his poor self-esteem led him to perceive failure at every turn. The somnolent conscience of 12 months previous now became a cruel and inflexible taskmaster, demanding perfection and punishing him with massive guilt when he delivered anything less. For a six month period he attempted to alleviate the depression with hallucinatory drugs and barbiturates. These served only to trigger his guilt and then require expiation by some further form of self-punishment. The first period of residential treatment ended at 20 months when Jerry elected to leave the hospital. For the preceding six months he had attempted a relationship with a girl: upon its failure he suffered depression so extreme that he could not perform in school and his very presence in the Adolescent Unit was a reminder of failure. He was discharged, took a job in his home town, and after six months, applied for readmission to the Adolescent Unit. In his letter inquiring about readmission he wrote:

> I am asking about the possibility of my coming to the Unit for further treatment and summer school. I feel I need its school, its therapy, and its therapeutic atmosphere. I started off this year in the tenth grade but never finished, and, of course, I realize it's no one's fault but mine. I've thought of summer school in other places, but feel nothing can beat the fact that it's better to start directly where I left off. It's important for me to work with the same teachers and the same school. And therapy. After being out of the hospital, in New York at times, and now at home, I've experienced what it's really like to make decisions concerning my life, which I've never made before even though I've run away, been away to military school, and, at times stayed at the hospital of my own will. For twenty months I have seen (at least this is how I feel) only how I react in the hospital with my hang-ups. Now I've seen how it is on the outside and I'm not happy with the reactions within myself to situations, especially in communicating with people. Actually, I'm quite happy with my progress through therapy. I do see myself doing better but I do see my mistakes and hang-ups. I spend a lot of time thinking about therapy and I cannot think differently, that is, as far as changing my mind to *not* having therapy. Actually, to sum things up, I have an overall feeling of incompleteness. I guess you see this and I hope you can help me out.

Jerry was readmitted and spent an additional nine months in residence. He applied himself to the same issues—his depression, the development and maintenance of relationships, the pervasive guilt and poor self-esteem, and his unrealistic aspirations about perfection. During this time Jerry passed the high school equivalency examination, and he left the hospital with this certificate and plans for a temporary job before attending college in the fall. At this writing, four years have elapsed since Jerry was admitted. At 19, in his first year of college, he contends with the same doubts and fears, but their strength has diminished and his self-control and insight are much improved. He is a functional and productive young man whose personal difficulties now have merged with problems which are endemic to his age group—heterosexual intimacy, choosing and preparing for vocation, and the broader questions of identity, as well as the purpose and meaning of life.

References

Becker, J., Iwakami, E. (1969). "Conflict and dominance within families of disturbed children," *Journal of Abnormal Psychology, 74,* 330–335.

Bower, E.M. (1966). "Personality and individual social maladjustment," in W.W. Wattenberg (Ed.), *Social Deviancy Among Youth.* 65th Yearbook of the NSSE, Part I, Chicago: Univ. of Chicago Press 103–134.

Brendtro, L. K. (1960). "Establishing relationship beachheads," in A.E. Trieschman, J.K. Whittaker, and L. K. Brendtro (Eds.), *The Other 23 Hours,* Chicago: Aldine.

Brochure. (1971). *Adolescent Unit,* John Umstead Hospital, Butner, N.C.

Brodie, R.D., and Winterbottom, M.R. (1967). "Failure in elementary school boys as a function of traumata, secrecy and derogation," *Child Development, 38,* 701–711.

Kohlberg, L. (1966). "Moral education in the schools: a developmental view," *The School Review, 74,* 1–30.

Related Reading

Bettelheim, B. (1957). *Truants From Life,* Glencoe, Ill.: Free Press.

Combs, A.W. (Ed.) (1962). *Perceiving, Behaving, Becoming,* Washington, D.C.: Association for Supervision and Curriculum Development, NEA.

Erikson, E.E. (1968). *Identity, Youth and Crisis,* New York: Norton.

Long, N.J., Morse, W.C., and Newman, R.G. (1965). *Conflict in the Classroom: The Education of Emotionally Disturbed Children,* Belmont, Calif. Wadsworth.

Newman, R.S. (1961). "Conveying essential messages to the emotionally disturbed child at school," *Exceptional Children, 28,* 199–204.

Noffsinger, T. (1968). "The effects of reward and level of aspiration in students with deviant behavior," *Exceptional Children, 37,* 355–364.

Redl, F. (1959). "The concept of the life space interview," *American Journal of Orthopsychiatry, 29,* 1–18.

Redl, F., and Wineman, D. (1957). *The Aggressive Child,* Glencoe, Ill.: Free Press.

Trieschman, A.E., and Whittaker, J.K., and Brendtro, L.K. (Eds.) (1969). *The Other 23 Hours,* Chicago: Aldine.

Wattenberg, W.W. (Ed.) (1966). *Social Deviancy Among Youth,* 65th Yearbook of the NSSE, Part 1, Chicago: Univ. of Chicago Press.

CHAPTER 11

Review of Cases

MAURICE F. FREEHILL

The cases presented here are typical but not proportionately represented. Moreover, they are cases that received treatment more intense than average. This bias is built in by the selection of authors. The cases were written by successful mental health workers about children who were well known because they had received much interest and care.

CHARACTERISTICS OF THE GROUP

Ordinarily, boys dominate treatment groups and are referred at earlier ages than girls. They may be more vulnerable, more exposed to stress, more readily viewed as disturbed or simply more disturbing. The general view is that only a few behaviors are sex-linked whereas many are sex related, influenced by role assignment and differential experience. In 10 cases, we might predict that seven or eight would be boys but this group deviates both in sex distribution and age. There are five girls, 4 to 12 years at inception of treatment and five boys, 9 to 17. Reasons for referral are more representative with three boys and only one girl referred chiefly for antisocial or disruptive behavior.

The children discussed come from three countries

and the Americans, from six states. Economic-cultural backgrounds appear to range from "deprived" to upper middle class. The problems include pseudo-retardation, autism, delinquency, defective self-concept with deficits in learning, and selective passive aggression. Treatment settings include hospital, residential, outpatient, educational, and consultative arrangements. The mental health agents include three who have primary identification with special education, three psychiatrists, four psychologists with teaching backgrounds, two psychologists with clinical or institutional experience, and a social worker. With one exception, it is relatively difficult to connect a case description with an author's professional specialty.

None of these children was treated in a community mental health center or was given service through volunteers, aides, or paraprofessionals. This is atypical. Following the Community Mental Health Centers Act in 1963, these centers became a major resource in the United States and there are similar services in Canada. The centers offer treatment and ally themselves with other agencies, thereby being available to a large percentage of all children. The centers also use volunteer and paraprofessional workers (as do other agencies). Beyond the school, the mental health center and its staff are the most common mental health agents for children.

Most of the methodologies are blends. For example, Elliott in chapter 9, and Marine in 6, make a good deal of conjunction between dynamic and operant models, while Stott's report on Jean and Wicklund's report on Helen are relatively pure applications. Most mental health workers choose a guiding model but are aware of and incorporate others under special circumstances for particular subpurposes.

Freud predicted that analysis would be modified to meet the needs of the poor and that popularity of psychoanalysis would compel combinations of this method with suggestion, hypnosis, and other forms of treatment. A behaviorist spokesman has recently pointed out that the form of therapy must be chosen by the therapist but efficiency calls for therapeutic flexibility (Lazarus, 1971). Lazarus thinks it is unfortunate that behavioral methods have acquired a modern glamour which results in indiscriminate use. He says that such methods have merit used properly in selected cases but outside their legitimate terrain they face failure.

DISTURBED ENVIRONMENTS

Children grow by building out from undifferentiated and egocentric responses. They differentiate one set of circumstances from another and above all, learn to know "me" from "not me." Loving and attentive parents adapt both object and person environments to provide stimulation and positive feedback for a child. In disturbed families, parents may be absorbed in personal anxieties and are inattentive to the child or they may restrict experience and deny growth in selected areas. So, we find a child like Mike who gets confused feedback. His hearing defect adds to highly inconsistent and vacillating responses from parents. His fantasy of voyaging in unknown space is analogous to his life in Toledo.

Kristen's world is almost incomprehensible. How is she to interpret her father's behavior, so unlike the behavior of other fathers? What echoes from father's problems or from mother's defective relationship with her own father enter into family conversations or stimulate attention or prompt a disguised reinforcement for Kristen's misbehavior? The mother, in some way, seemed fulfilled when the problem was declared too big for the family. Would removal from the home satisfy some compulsive wish or only complete an expectation? This is a powerful and sad example of disturbed communication among disturbed people.

Barry, too, responded to ambiguous messages. Mr.

Knowles was unaware that he sent them and they were not understood by his family. The treatment was operant, but the efficacy of treatment was elevated through reinterpretation of Mr. Knowles' handicap as an influence in family interactions.

Damaging effects from unresponsive environments have many manifestations. Morse and Ketcham (1965) have shown that high organismic potential with constructive school and home conditions lead to high achievement and high adjustment while the same potential with detrimental conditions results in high achievement with low adjustment. For those with low organismic potential, constructive nurture produces low achievement with high adjustment while detrimental nurture results in both low achievement and adjustment.

Detrimental conditions are often associated with influence problems (Brodie and Winterbottom, 1967). Since children learn so much about themselves from others, they are handicapped if adults cannot share, cannot tolerate growth and independence, or are disturbed by relationships with the child.

Whole cultures may be unresponsive. In mass society, the individual identifies with a subgroup and relinquishes decision-making and authority to his union, corporation, or cult. Bureaucracy supports impersonal and categorical interactions reducing personal significance and responsibility. School organization may reflect the urban and business structure, better suited to industry than to nurture.

To escape impersonality, the individual searches out personal meaning, often in the family. Here, too, he may find limited contact, little enjoyment of others, unsteady influences from one generation to another, and in the extreme, there may be severe pathology. Johnny's father had a stubborn pride that reduced his chances to communicate with his children. Tina was cast in the role of "dummy" to meet her sister's needs and to help her mother deal with old insults. The

Glover "parent-selves" left little place for a child. Jerry aroused his father's hostility by interfering with professional success, and he activated Mrs. Glover's sense of anxiety and resentment about her own inadequacies. Jerry learned anger and struggle, and perhaps because he was small, he learned to simulate compliance. With increasing size his efforts to subdue and humiliate spread outside the home and became less tolerable.

POSITIVE MENTAL HEALTH

A case orientation puts emphasis on the troubled child and reduces attention to positive mental health. Nevertheless, three decades ago, case materials placed more emphasis on enuresis, stuttering, memory faults, and pathology and less on coping behavior. Positive mental health implies accomplishment, personal-soundness and ability to manage stress. There is no universal set of positive criteria. Adjustment often appears to be viewed as achieving external acceptability at the price of internal harmony. Treatment for Jerry most clearly demonstrates an effort to go beyond conforming-to-please, in order to achieve autonomous and self-fulfilling behavior.

Therapeutic services cannot overlook pathology. To be mentally healthy, a client must perceive reality and distinguish between objective harm and archaic frustrations as Kristen could not. Testing reality is difficult if experience is restricted by cultural fragmentation as it was for Ken or by ambiguous and contorted experience with parents as it was with Jerry. In all cases, reality is modified by self-assessment. A positive self-acceptance is not just a benign unfolding of self-regard, but at least partly something learned from mutual process and reflective valuations. The self-image may be distorted by identification with a pathological family or by failure or sense of failure to become an approved person—a syndrome clearly evident in Helen and Mike.

Contemporary psychologists try to do more than relieve pathology. The people who worked with Jean, Susan, and Tina deliberately influenced ways of behaving. Positive mental health is not value-free, it teaches specifics in functioning and perceiving (Smith, 1961). High among the values are social competencies and interpersonal skills. For example, Jean had to learn not only some measure of independence but appropriate ways of managing reasonable dependence.

The goals of overcoming and accomplishing are not separated. In all but the case of Kristen (and perhaps Ken) these children have been liberated from archaic fears or damaging habits which previously limited development. Improved behavior, stronger relationships, and more buoyant self have increased their options enlarging both achievement and emotional potentials. In school or in clinic, the issue is curriculum *and* climate not curriculum *or* climate (Wertheimer, 1971).

Availability of numerous and far-reaching choices increase an individual's freedom but also enhance responsibility and commitment. One who sees himself as a failure or as a victim is unable to accept responsibilities. Laboratory or "T-Group" methods are often advocated as a means to help the person acquire interpersonal skills, understand discrepancies in his own perception, and realize that he does influence others. In human relations training, responsibility is viewed as response-ability, a capacity to respond in highly personalized fashion (Perls, 1969).

Some people would limit mental health goals to inculcating what is proper and training what is useful. At least, they would argue that public monies should not be spent to establish individuality. Nevertheless, character, creativity, and scholarship depend on high personalization. From observations in concentration camps, Bettelheim concluded that essential courage was accompanied by a conscious freedom, a conviction that one still had some command, some influence, an ability to draw a line beyond which no other could influence his inner life (Bettelheim, 1960). So, too, creative persons are found to be personal with a childlike relation between themselves and their work. They have a stubborn belief in the rightness of what they do. They offer audacious challenge to conditioning, stereotyped beliefs, and to their own experiences.

THE NATURE OF TREATMENT

This volume touches on a variety of treatment methodologies—individual, family and group counseling, as well as remedial education in several patterns. Variety is the *status quo.* Morse, Cutler, and Fink (1964) surveyed special classes for the disturbed in 54 school systems. They found many relatively untrained teachers, a general goal of return to regular classes, and a wide divergence in models. Educational patterns with restriction and corrective tutorial attention and "psycho-educational" patterns with a balance of teaching and therapy were common. There were "engineered" classrooms managed by a learning specialist using operant methods and emphasizing associative training. Some were "psychodynamic", others "naturalistic (depending on healthy interaction between teacher and child) or "primitive" (allowing child expression).

Because this is a brief book and because authors were invited to write cases that illustrate important principles, other matters may seem slighted. All of us are interested in young children, transient problems and ordinary school services. Schools are next to homes in both developmental and remedial services. Counselors and teachers work in much the same fashion as the authors in this volume. In recent years experts have been used as consultants working less in direct service and more in the enhancement of indispensible services given by teachers, counselors and aides (Newman, 1967; Caplan 1970).

Schools try to provide a positive atmosphere and curriculum which promotes personal growth. Some schools and clinics have made special inclusions, or modified content to give attention to interpersonal and psychic development. The best known of these efforts is the work of Ralph Ojemann out of the State University of Iowa. Traditional subject matter is handled to exploit understanding of dynamic and interpersonal relations. From 20 years of data, Ojemann (1967) reports success in reducing anxiety, arbitrary punitiveness, and antidemocratic tendencies while enlarging tolerance for ambiguity and improving perceptions of authority. Other approaches are found in the work of Rokeach and Rotter. Rokeach (1971) has studied the development of values or central beliefs which become internalized guides to action and Rotter (1971) has experimented with the development of trust and the positively associated qualities of trustworthiness.

The case evidence supports other studies in the conclusion that effective help is individualized, structured, lengthy, and empathic (Bednar and Weinberg, 1970). Growth seems sometimes to be blunted from a particular instant but remediation comes slowly. Positive mental health is a complex and long-term achievement.

References

Bedner, R.L., and Weinberg, S.L. (1970). "Ingredients of successful treatment programs for underachievers," *Journal of Counseling Psychology, 17,* 17.

Bettelheim, B. (1960). *The Informed Heart,* Glencoe, Ill.: The Free Press.

Brodie, R.D., and Winterbottom, M.R. (1967). "Failure in elementary school boys as a function of traumata, secrecy and derogation," *Child Development, 38,* 701–711.

Caplan, G. (1970). *The Theory and Practice of Mental Health Consultation,* New York: Basic Books.

Lazarus, A.A. (1971). *Behavior Therapy and Beyond,* New York: McGraw-Hill.

Morse, W.C., Cutler, R.L., and Fink, A.H. (1964). *Public School Classes for the Emotionally Handicapped: A Research Analysis,* Washington, D.C.: C.E.C., Nat. Education Assoc.

Morse, W.C., and Ketcham, W.A. (1965). *Dimensions of Children's Social and Psychological Development Related to School Achievement,* Co-op. Res. Project, No. 1286, Ann Arbor: University of Michigan.

Newman, R. (1967). *Psychological Consultation in the Schools,* New York: Basic Books.

Ojemann, R.H. (1967). "Incorporating psychological concepts in the school curriculum," *Journal of School Psychology, 5,* 195–204.

Perls, F.S. (1969). *Gestalt Therapy Verbatim,* Lafayette, Calif.: Real People Press.

Rokeach, M. (1971). "Long-range experimental modification of values, attitudes and behaviors," *American Psychologist, 26,* 453–459.

Rotter, J.B. (1971). "Generalized expectancies for interpersonal trust," *American Psychologist, 26,* 443–452.

Smith, M.B. (1961). "Mental health reconsidered: a special case of the problem of values in psychology," *American Psychologist, 16,* 229–306.

Wertheimer, P.A. (1971). "School climate and student learning," *Phi Delta Kappan, 51,* 527–530.

Author Index

Subject Index